Business Intelligence for Higher Education

Azwa Abdul Aziz • Julaily Aida Jusoh •
Wan Suryani Wan Awang

# Business Intelligence for Higher Education

## Empowering Data-Driven Decision Making

Springer

Azwa Abdul Aziz
Universiti Sultan Zainal Abidin
Besut, Malaysia

Julaily Aida Jusoh
Universiti Sultan Zainal Abidin
Besut, Malaysia

Wan Suryani Wan Awang
Universiti Sultan Zainal Abidin
Besut, Malaysia

ISBN 978-3-032-05360-2 ISBN 978-3-032-05361-9 (eBook)
https://doi.org/10.1007/978-3-032-05361-9



This Springer imprint is published by the registered company Springer Nature Switzerland AG
The registered company address is: Gewerbestrasse 11, 6330 Cham, Switzerland

# Preface

In an era marked by rapid digital transformation, higher education institutions (HEIs) increasingly recognize the strategic value of Business Intelligence (BI) in refining and strengthening decision-making processes. Effective decision-making powered by comprehensive data analytics is now pivotal for addressing critical areas such as student enrollment trends, academic performance monitoring, financial planning, resource allocation, and overall institutional strategy. The ability to harness data-driven insights has emerged as essential for ensuring operational efficiency, maintaining competitive advantage, and achieving sustainable growth within academia.

This book, titled "Business Intelligence for Higher Education: Empowering Data-Driven Decision Making," provides a robust, comprehensive, and interdisciplinary exploration of BI as applied specifically to the higher education sector. By bridging the traditional approaches of academic administration with contemporary analytical methodologies, the book clearly illustrates how BI tools, technologies, and strategic frameworks can significantly optimize institutional performance and drive educational innovation.

Purpose and Scope: This text serves as a foundational resource aimed at higher education administrators, educators, researchers, and policymakers eager to effectively leverage the transformative capabilities of BI. The content delves into both theoretical and practical dimensions, covering technological innovations, analytical strategies, and real-world applications of BI. Additionally, readers will find comprehensive discussions on best practices for data governance, predictive analytics, and machine learning, designed explicitly to bolster student success, operational effectiveness, and institutional advancement.

Target Audience: This book is primarily crafted for:

- University and institutional leaders, administrators, and policymakers committed to strategic improvement through data insights
- Academics and researchers with a keen interest in advancing educational data analytics

- IT and data professionals tasked with developing and managing robust institutional data infrastructures
- Graduate students enrolled in programs focused on business intelligence, data analytics, and educational management who are preparing to lead data-driven initiatives

Besut, Malaysia Azwa Abdul Aziz
Besut, Malaysia Julaily Aida Jusoh
Besut, Malaysia Wan Suryani Wan Awang

**Competing Interests** The authors have no competing interests to declare that are relevant to the content of this manuscript.

# Contents


**1 Business Intelligence in Higher Education** ... 1
1.1 Introduction ... 1
1.2 Challenges of Business Intelligence Implementation in Higher Education ... 7
1.3 Case Study: Successful Implementations of BI in Higher Education Institutions ... 13
1.4 Chapter Conclusion ... 15

**2 Data Governance and Management** ... 17
2.1 Introduction ... 17
2.2 Data Quality (DQ) ... 18
2.3 Measuring DQ ... 19
2.4 Data Quality Process ... 20
2.5 Chapter Conclusion ... 24

**3 BI Tools and Technologies for Higher Education** ... 27
3.1 Introduction ... 27
3.2 Components and Techniques of BI Tools ... 28
3.3 Categories of BI Platforms ... 36
3.4 Applying BI tools in Higher Education ... 38
3.5 Chapter Conclusion ... 40

**4 Building a Data Warehouse for Higher Education** ... 43
4.1 Introduction ... 43
4.2 Data Warehouse (DW) ... 43
4.3 Extract Transformation Load (ETL) ... 53
4.4 Building Educational Data Warehouse (EDW) ... 54
4.5 Chapter Conclusion ... 58

**5 Data Visualization and Reporting** ... 61
5.1 Introduction ... 61
5.2 The Importance of Data Visualization ... 61
5.3 Dashboard Design Principles ... 62

5.4 Key Performance Indicators (KPI) . . . 66
5.5 Chapter Conclusion . . . 74

**6 Enhancing Student Success with BI** . . . 77
6.1 Introduction . . . 77
6.2 Implementing BI for Student Success (Malaysian Case Study for ICT Sector) . . . 78
6.3 Chapter Conclusion . . . 87

**7 Privacy, Security, and Ethical Considerations** . . . 89
7.1 Introduction . . . 89
7.2 Safeguarding Student and Institutional Data in a BI Environment . . . 90
7.3 Best Practices for Safeguarding Student and Institutional Data . . . 93
7.4 Compliance with Data Protection Regulations (e.g., GDPR, HIPAA) . . . 94
7.5 Chapter Conclusion . . . 97

**8 Future Trends in BI for Higher Education** . . . 99
8.1 Introduction . . . 99
8.2 Emerging Technologies in Higher Education . . . 100
8.3 Predictions of BI Future in the Academic Sector . . . 106
8.4 Chapter Conclusion . . . 107

**References** . . . 109

# Chapter 1
# Business Intelligence in Higher Education

## 1.1 Introduction

Data analytics is the process of examining, cleaning, transforming, and interpreting data to uncover meaningful patterns, trends, and insights that support decision-making and problem-solving. It involves working with data from multiple sources, including structured formats such as databases and spreadsheets, as well as unstructured data like text, images, and videos, to draw conclusions or make predictions. By leveraging data analytics, organizations and individuals can make informed decisions, enhance operational efficiency, mitigate risks, foster innovation, and achieve strategic goals. In various sectors—such as business, education, healthcare, and public policy—data analytics has become a critical enabler of evidence-based practices and continuous improvement.

As digital transformation accelerates, the ability to use data effectively is no longer optional; it is a core competency. The integration of analytics into daily operations helps organizations personalize services, anticipate future trends, and respond rapidly to changes. Tools powered by artificial intelligence and machine learning have further expanded the capabilities of analytics, enabling real-time insights and predictive capabilities that drive proactive strategies. This evolution is especially significant in education and research, where data-driven approaches now support everything from curriculum design and student engagement to institutional planning and performance measurement.

Business Intelligence (BI), a key domain within data analytics, refers to a set of strategies, technologies, and tools that transform raw data into actionable insights to inform business decisions. BI encompasses a range of functions, including data visualization, dashboards, online analytical processing (OLAP), and reporting systems, enabling users to explore historical and current data in a meaningful way. Through BI, organizations can monitor key performance indicators (KPIs), identify inefficiencies, and uncover opportunities for innovation and improvement. It



A. A. Aziz et al., *Business Intelligence for Higher Education*,
https://doi.org/10.1007/978-3-032-05361-9_1

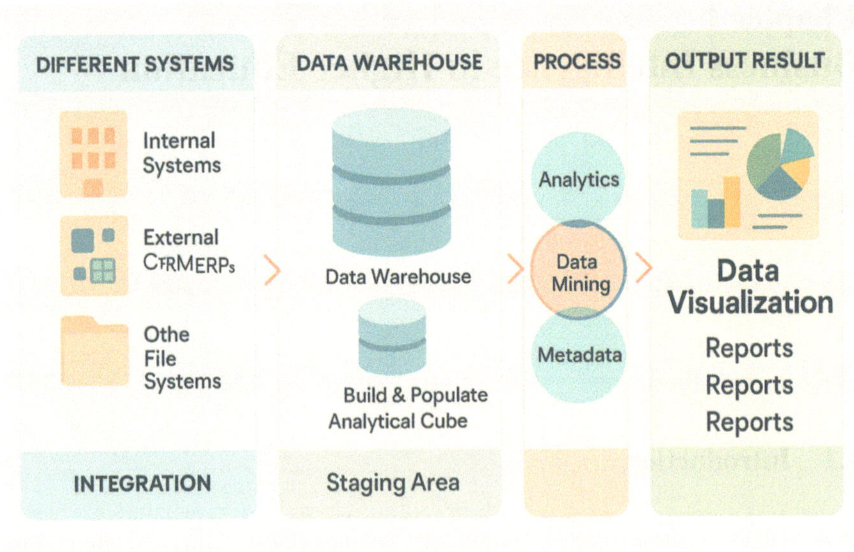


**Fig. 1.1** BI structure

provides a centralized view of data across departments, promoting collaboration and alignment with strategic goals.

In the context of higher education, BI is increasingly adopted to support academic performance monitoring, student retention strategies, financial forecasting, and resource allocation. Institutions utilize BI platforms to identify at-risk students, optimize course schedules, and ensure compliance with accreditation standards. By enabling timely and evidence-based decisions, BI helps educational institutions navigate challenges and maintain a competitive edge in a rapidly evolving landscape. As educational data becomes more complex and voluminous, the role of BI in translating that data into insights that support teaching, learning, and administration becomes more indispensable than ever.

BI refers to the wide variety of data analysis methodologies, tools, and strategies that enable the transformation of unprocessed data into meaningful and actionable insights. The fundamental aim of business intelligence is to transform the data into actionable information, helping organizations and institutions to make better decisions, indicate opportunities, and solve issues more effectively. Figure 1.1 shows the standard framework for BI structure process.

Here are some key various significant components and qualities that deserve to be reviewed further regarding BI.

### 1.1.1 Data Layer

The data layer serves as the fundamental framework that underpins the entire BI system. It covers a wide range of processes, technologies and infrastructures dedicated to collection storage processing and the management of data for analytical purposes. The significance of the data layer lies in its direct influence on the quality, accessibility, and usability of the data utilized for BI analysis and reporting. The key components of the data layer in business intelligence include:

#### 1.1.1.1 Data Sources

Data is collected from a variety of systems, applications, databases, and sources, which may originate either internally or externally to an organization. Internal data sources refer to any system or repository within the organization that generates data as part of routine operations. Examples include transactional databases that record business activities such as sales and purchases, Customer Relationship Management (CRM) systems that manage interactions with clients and prospects, and Enterprise Resource Planning (ERP) systems that integrate functions like finance, human resources, and supply chain management.

On the other hand, external data sources involve systems or repositories outside the organization. These sources provide data that complements internal information and supports a broad range of analytical and strategic purposes. External data is valuable for understanding market dynamics, customer behavior, competitive benchmarks, and other external influences on business performance. Common examples include social media platforms (such as Twitter and Facebook) for sentiment and engagement insights, web analytics tools (like Google Analytics) for tracking website traffic and user behavior, and datasets provided by third-party vendors offering industry-specific intelligence.

Together, these internal and external data sources form an integral part of the organization's data ecosystem. They are harnessed in business intelligence processes to enable comprehensive analysis, enhance strategic planning, and support data-driven decision-making.

#### 1.1.1.2 Data Integration

Organizations today deal with information coming from many different places—such as internal systems, databases, apps, and even external sources like social media or data from outside companies. Since these sources often use different formats and ways of organizing information, it can be difficult to combine and analyze everything smoothly. To make this possible, the data needs to be brought together in a consistent and organized way.

This process starts with cleaning the data, which means fixing mistakes, filling in missing details, removing duplicates, and making sure everything is written in a clear and standard format. Once the data is clean, the next step is transforming it, which involves reshaping or converting it so that it fits well with the tools and systems the organization uses to analyze data. This might include grouping similar data together or doing simple calculations.

Another important step is organizing the data properly, often by arranging it into simpler, more connected pieces to avoid confusion or repeated information. This helps keep the data accurate and easy to manage. When all of these steps—cleaning, transforming, and organizing—are done well, the result is a clear and reliable set of information that the organization can use for deeper analysis and better decision-making.

By integrating data in this way, organizations ensure that everyone is working with the same information, reduce the chance of mistakes, and gain clearer insights that support smarter strategies and actions.

## *1.1.2 Presentation Layer*

In BI, the presentation layer refers to the interface through which users interact with and consume insights derived from data analysis. It serves as the front-end component of a BI system, responsible for presenting data in a visually appealing and comprehensible format to facilitate decision-making and strategic planning. Additionally, it also plays a crucial role in delivering actionable insights to users by presenting data in a format that is intuitive, informative, and tailored to their specific needs and preferences. It serves as the interface through which users interact with BI tools and leverage data analysis to drive informed decision-making and achieve business objectives. There are several key characteristics of the presentation layer in BI:

### 1.1.2.1 Reporting

BI solutions enable users to create queries and generate reports tailored to their specific needs. These reports can provide information at both high and granular levels, making them valuable for different stakeholders. Reports are structured documents that summarize and present data analysis findings in a standardized format. These documents serve as a vital tool in business intelligence (BI) by presenting information in a clear, organized manner, facilitating informed decision-making across various levels of an organization. They may include tables, charts, graphs, and textual descriptions to communicate insights effectively. Reports can be scheduled for regular distribution or generated on-demand to support decision-making at various levels of the organization.

#### 1.1.2.2 Dashboards

A BI dashboard serves as a centralized platform for aggregating and displaying pertinent data in a visually appealing and user-friendly style. Dashboards are customizable, interactive interfaces that provide users with a visual overview of key performance indicators (KPIs), metrics, and trends relevant to their specific roles or objectives. Dashboards typically consist of charts, graphs, gauges, and other visualizations that enable users to monitor performance, track progress, and identify areas requiring attention in real-time. By presenting data into simple charts, graphs, and tables, BI dashboards facilitate users to swiftly analyse trends, discover patterns, as well as gain insightful knowledge into their organization's performance throughout departments and functions. It also includes customisation possibilities, allowing users to adjust the display of certain indicators or KPIs based on their preferences and the objectives of the organization. Users may customize the dashboard to focus on the parameters that are most important to them, such as tracking sales numbers, monitoring inventory levels, or analysing customer happiness scores. Interactivity is an important component of BI dashboards, allowing users to engage with data and further explore insights. Users can delve down into certain points of data, filter information in accordance with their interests, and do ad hoc research studies that provide more depth of understanding. This interactive functionality enables users to figure out the complexity behind the statistics and make educated decisions based on a thorough grasp of the facts. On top of that, BI dashboards frequently include real-time or near-real-time data updates to guarantee that the information shown is accurate as it reflects the most recent events inside the organization. This data timeliness permits users to respond immediately to changing conditions and confidently make data-driven decisions.

#### 1.1.2.3 Ad Hoc Analysis

Ad hoc analysis refers to BI systems' capability to allow users to execute real-time data analysis. This sort of analysis allows users to freely explore data and answer individual questions rather than depending on pre-defined reports or structured queries. Ad hoc analysis allows users to interact with data interactively, adjust various parameters, apply filters, and view findings in real time. This enables users to explore trends, observe patterns, and learn insights that are not readily obvious in regular or pre-built reports.

#### 1.1.2.4 Predictive Analytics

Predictive analytics is another form of BI that comprises advanced statistical techniques, machine learning algorithms, and predictive modelling for predicting future trends, events, or behaviours based on prior information patterns. Predictive analytics allows organizations to accurately anticipate upcoming occurrences or trends and come up with predictive choices to boost business processes and performance. Predictive analytics techniques can make predictions about future occurrences through analysis of preceding data and understanding trends. In the case of sales forecasting, predictive analytics may utilize prior sale data, seasonality, market patterns, and economic indicators to forecast future sales rates. Conversely, in consumer behaviour analysis, predictive analytics can use previous customer interactions, purchase history, demographics, and other pertinent data to forecast future customer preferences, purchasing habits, or churn likelihood.

#### 1.1.2.5 Data Visualization and Decision Support

Data visualization is an important aspect of BI systems that includes transforming raw data into intriguing charts, graphs, and interactive representations. These visualizations serve an important role in interpreting complicated statistics and successfully communicating insights to users. Data visualization supports the analysis of patterns, trends, and relationships within data by illustrating it in a visual manner, allowing users to analyse and analyse it easily. Visualizations are effective methods for improving data understanding due to their leverage human visual perception, which is capable of spotting patterns and trends. Users may immediately acquire essential insights and comprehend the underlying relationships within data via graphical representations, eliminating the need for complex numerical analysis. The ability to visually study data enables users to discover relevant insights and make educated decisions based on a better comprehension of the facts. Decision support is a vital component of BI that provides decision-makers with the information and insights required to make accurate decisions across many sectors of the organization, including operations, marketing, finance, and others as well. Decision-makers may use BI systems to access a range of data sources, including real-time and historical data, performing analysis and create reports or dashboards that highlight KPIs and trends important to their decision-making processes. BI systems offer decision-makers access to a unified platform from which they can retrieve and analyse data from multiple sources inside the organization. This consists of data regarding sales, consumer behaviour, financial performance, inventory levels, and more. By integrating data from multiple sources into a unified interface, BI systems provide decision-makers with a complete perspective of the organization's performance among departments and functions. Decision-makers can analyse real-time or historical data to detect patterns, trends, and correlations. This study assists decision-makers with comprehending the elements driving company performance, allowing them to make data-driven decisions that promote corporate development and success. Decision-makers may obtain a deeper knowledge of data and generate actionable insights that will help them make better decisions by utilizing data visualization tools within BI systems. Whether it's discovering areas for improvement, optimizing processes, or figuring out growth prospects, business intelligence provides decision-makers with the knowledge they need to effectively drive strategic efforts and achieve corporate goals.

In general, BI is essential for businesses of all sizes and sectors, allowing them to use their data for competitive advantage, operational efficiency, and growth. In today's fast-paced corporate climate, BI allows for data-driven decision-making and strategic initiatives by gathering, analysing, and interpreting data from many sources. It compiles data into a centralized platform, providing a complete picture of operations, customers, and market trends. The benefits of business intelligence include the ability to make educated decisions based on data insights, to optimize performance using KPIs, and to facilitate strategic planning using predictive analytics.

## 1.2 Challenges of Business Intelligence Implementation in Higher Education

Business Intelligence (BI) is increasingly becoming a transformative force in higher education, offering institutions the tools to make informed, data-driven decisions across academic and administrative domains. As universities and colleges navigate the complexities of enrollment management, student retention, financial planning, and institutional accountability, BI provides timely insights through data collection, analysis, and visualization. It enables decision-makers to assess trends, measure performance, and allocate resources more strategically, fostering a culture of evidence-based management within academia.

In the academic sphere, BI plays a crucial role in improving student success and educational quality. By analyzing performance indicators such as grades, attendance, and learning engagement, institutions can identify students who may be struggling and offer timely support or interventions. This approach supports personalized learning, where teaching methods and resources are adapted to suit individual student needs. Moreover, educators can use BI-generated insights to refine teaching strategies, optimize curriculum design, and ensure learning objectives are effectively met.

Operationally, BI enhances institutional efficiency by helping manage financial resources, physical infrastructure, and human capital more effectively. Institutions can use BI tools to monitor expenditures, forecast budgets, and identify cost-saving opportunities. Facilities can be better managed by analyzing usage patterns to ensure optimal scheduling and reduce waste. Integrating data from departments such as admissions, finance, and student services into a centralized system allows institutions to break down silos and achieve a cohesive view of their performance, enabling more coordinated and informed strategic planning.

Additionally, BI supports higher education institutions in meeting regulatory and accreditation requirements by streamlining the reporting process and ensuring data accuracy. Automated reporting features reduce manual effort and minimize errors, providing institutions with up-to-date information for audits and compliance reviews. Furthermore, BI helps universities identify emerging trends in student demographics, market needs, and graduate outcomes, allowing them to align academic offerings with labor market demands. In this way, BI not only improves institutional effectiveness but also supports long-term growth, relevance, and competitiveness in an evolving educational landscape.

Implementing BI in the higher education sector can provide numerous advantages, but it also presents a set of challenges. The keys challenges in introducing BI in Higher Education are illustrates in Fig. 1.2.

## *1.2.1 Data-Driven Decision Making*

Data-driven decision-making in education involves using data to plan effectively and monitor and enhance the performance of both students and educators. In the context of education, it requires two main aspects:

- Proactive Planning: BI tools help educational institutions analyse historical data to make informed decisions for future planning and resource allocation. Educational institutions utilize Business Intelligence (BI) tools to examine data from the past, enabling them to make well-informed decisions for the future. By studying historical enrolment data, the institution can predict future student numbers, allowing them to plan faculty resources, classroom space, and other necessities accordingly.
- Performance Monitoring: Schools can track student and teacher performance, identify trends, and implement strategies for improvement. Schools employ data analysis to keep track of how both students and teachers are performing. By analysing test scores and teacher evaluations over time, the institution can identify patterns or trends. This information can then be used to implement targeted

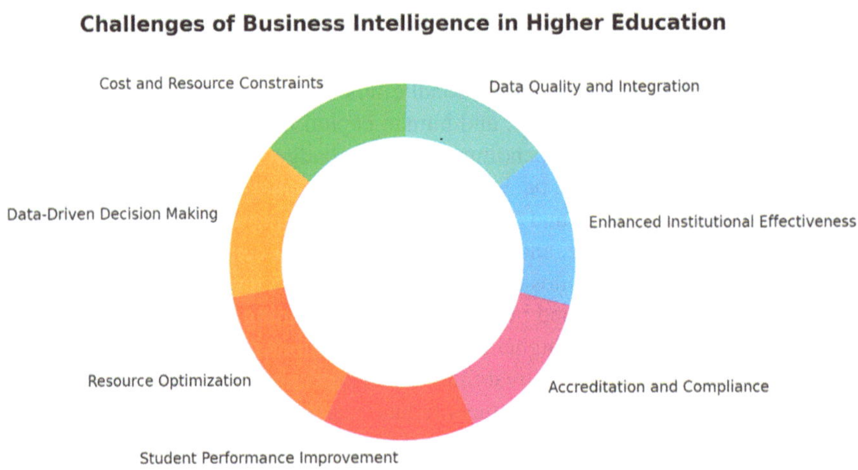


**Fig. 1.2** Challenges of business intelligence in higher education

strategies for improvement, such as additional support for struggling students or professional development for teachers.

### 1.2.2 Resource Optimization

In the educational environment, optimizing resources requires utilizing BI tools to strengthen the efficiency of resource management. Resource optimization in education involves leveraging BI tools to enhance financial decision-making and streamline the management of physical resources, ultimately contributing to better operational efficiency and reduced wastage. This includes two significant aspects:

- Financial Management: BI tools assist educational institutions in budgeting, forecasting, and analyzing financial data, helping educational institutions optimize resource allocation and reduce waste. By analyzing financial trends and expenditures, the institution can make informed decisions about budget allocation, identify areas for cost savings, and ensure financial stability.
- Facility Management: Efficiently manage resources like classrooms, facilities, and equipment to enhance overall operational efficiency. Efficiently overseeing and allocating physical resources such as classrooms, facilities, and equipment using data-driven insights. BI tools can help the institution analyze usage patterns of classrooms, ensuring optimal scheduling and usage. This can lead to better space utilization, reduced downtime, and improved overall operational efficiency.

### 1.2.3 Student Performance Improvement

Focusing on student performance improvement involves early detection of academic challenges through BI tools and implementing personalized learning strategies to address the unique needs of each student. This benefit encompasses two main strategies:

- Early Intervention: BI can identify students who may be at risk of falling behind, allowing for early intervention and targeted support. BI tools have the capability to identify students who may be at risk of academic challenges early, empowering institutions to intervene promptly and offer targeted support. By analysing diverse data points such as attendance records, test scores, and behavioural patterns, BI tools can pinpoint students who may require additional assistance. This early detection enables educators to implement customized interventions like tutoring, counselling, or personalized learning plans.
- Personalized Learning: Tailor teaching methods based on data insights to address the unique needs of individual students. By utilizing insights derived from data analysis, educators can tailor teaching methods to meet the unique learning

requirements of individual students. Through the examination of student performance data, educators can pinpoint particular areas where students may require extra support or stimulation. Subsequently, they can modify teaching approaches, materials, and pacing to align more closely with each student's learning style and pace, thereby fostering improved academic development and engagement.

### 1.2.4 Accreditation and Compliance

In higher education, it entails the utilization of BI tools to oversee regulatory standards and streamline the reporting process. This ensures that educational institutions fullfill accreditation requirements in a more efficient and accurate manner. This advantage comprises two main components:

- Regulatory Compliance: BI tools assist higher educational institutions in monitoring and ensuring compliance with regulatory standards and accreditation criteria. These tools can monitor a range of regulatory requirements, including student-teacher ratios, curriculum standards, and safety regulations. It provides insights and notifications to assist institutions in upholding compliance with these standards, thereby preventing penalties and safeguarding their accreditation status.
- Automated Reporting: Automating the collection and analysis of data required for accreditation reports using Business Intelligence (BI) tools streamlines the entire reporting process within educational institutions. This automation significantly reduces the time and effort needed to compile and analyse data, thereby saving valuable resources for staff members. Moreover, by minimizing manual intervention, the risk of human errors in reporting is greatly decreased. This ensures that the reports generated are accurate and up-to-date, meeting the stringent requirements of accreditation bodies. Furthermore, BI tools provide real-time insights into the data, allowing institutions to generate reports promptly as needed, without delays. This not only simplifies the accreditation process by ensuring timely submission of required documentation but also enables educational institutions to continuously monitor their compliance status. Overall, the automation facilitated by BI tools enhances the efficiency and reliability of the accreditation process, enabling institutions to maintain their accreditation status with ease.

### 1.2.5 Enhanced Institutional Effectiveness

It refers to the improvement of overall performance and achievement within an educational institution. Leveraging BI plays a pivotal role in achieving this by utilizing data-driven insights to inform strategic planning efforts and enhance communication with stakeholders. BI tools enable higher educational institutions to analyse vast amounts of data related to various aspects of operations, including enrolment trends, demographic shifts, student performance, resource allocation, and financial management. Besides, it also facilitates the collection, analysis, and visualization of data related to stakeholder engagement, including student feedback, parent surveys, alumni participation, and community involvement. By extracting valuable insights from this data, institutions can make informed decisions regarding long-term goals, resource allocation, program development, and operational improvements. BI analysis might reveal emerging trends in student preferences or shifts in demographic patterns, prompting institutions to adjust their offerings or allocate resources accordingly to stay competitive and meet the evolving needs of their stakeholders.

### *1.2.6 Data Quality and Integration*

It is the processes and practices involved in ensuring the accuracy, consistency, and integration of data across various systems and departments within the institution. The data quality and integration in higher educational institutions involve addressing challenges related to data silos, ensuring data accuracy, integrating data from various sources, and implementing robust data governance practices to support informed decision-making and improve institutional effectiveness. Addressing data silos and ensuring data accuracy are critical challenges that educational institutions face when leveraging Business Intelligence (BI) tools. Answering these difficulties enables institutions to integrate data from multiple sources, assure data quality, and obtain trustworthy insights for informed decision-making, eventually encouraging institutional progress and success.

- Data Silos: Higher educational institutions often maintain separate databases or systems for different functions such as student records, financial management, human resources, and academic research. These separate systems create data silos, where data is stored in isolated environments and not easily accessible or integrated with other systems. Data silos hinder the ability to gain a holistic view of institutional operations and performance. They also impede the integration of data from various sources, limiting the effectiveness of BI tools in providing comprehensive insights. Institutions can address data silos by implementing data integration strategies such as data warehousing, data lakes, or application programming interfaces (APIs). By consolidating data from multiple sources into a centralized repository, institutions can break down data silos and enable seamless data access and analysis.
- Data Accuracy: Ensuring the accuracy and consistency of data is crucial for obtaining reliable insights from BI tools. Data inaccuracies, inconsistencies, or errors can lead to incorrect analyses and unreliable decision-making. Inaccurate data can undermine the credibility of BI insights and result in flawed

decision-making. It can also erode trust in the BI system and impede its adoption by users. Institutions can ensure data accuracy through rigorous data quality management practices. This includes data validation, cleansing, and normalization processes to identify and correct errors or inconsistencies. Establishing data governance policies and standards can also help maintain data accuracy by defining data ownership, quality criteria, and data management procedures.

### *1.2.7 Cost and Resource Constraints*

To overcome cost and resource constraints in implementing BI in higher educational institutions, it's important to manage costs, find affordable solutions, and upgrade infrastructure. By addressing these challenges, institutions can maximize the value of BI tools and harness data-driven insights to improve decision-making and enhance institutional effectiveness.

- Implementation Costs: Acquiring and implementing BI tools can pose substantial financial challenges for higher educational institutions, particularly those operating with limited budgets. The significant upfront expenses associated with purchasing BI software licenses, hardware, and consulting services can impose strain on the financial resources of these institutions. Consequently, this may result in budgetary constraints and difficulties in allocating funds for BI implementation projects. To mitigate this challenge, educational institutions can explore various cost-effective BI solutions. For instance, opting for open-source software or leveraging cloud-based BI platforms can significantly reduce upfront costs and alleviate the burden on limited budgets. Open-source BI software offers flexible and customizable options without the need for expensive licensing fees, while cloud-based BI platforms provide scalable solutions that eliminate the need for substantial investments in on-premises infrastructure. Additionally, educational institutions can seek funding opportunities or grants specifically aimed at supporting technology investments, including BI implementation projects. By proactively exploring such avenues for financial support, institutions can offset implementation costs and ensure the successful adoption of BI tools within their budgetary constraints. The implementation of BI tools in educational institutions requires exploring cost-effective solutions, such as open-source software or cloud-based platforms, and actively seeking funding opportunities to offset implementation costs and facilitate the adoption of BI solutions within budget limitations.
- Infrastructure: The Higher Educational Institutions may require investment in upgrading their infrastructure and technology systems to effectively support the implementation and operation of BI tools. Challenges such as outdated hardware, limited network bandwidth, and inadequate data storage capacity can impede the performance and scalability of BI solutions. Integrating BI tools with existing systems and ensuring compatibility with legacy technology may also

pose challenges. To address these infrastructure constraints, institutions need to invest in hardware upgrades, network enhancements, and data storage solutions tailored to the requirements of BI implementation. Additionally, they may explore options such as outsourcing infrastructure management to third-party vendors or utilizing cloud-based BI platforms known for their scalability and flexibility.

## 1.3 Case Study: Successful Implementations of BI in Higher Education Institutions

BI solution has been successfully implemented at several higher education institutions in Europe. Here are some successful implementations of business intelligence (BI) in higher education institutions (Table 1.1):

The case studies presented highlight how prestigious universities across the globe have strategically implemented BI to tackle unique institutional challenges and enhance operational effectiveness.

At the University of California, Berkeley, BI was crucial in modernizing financial operations. By streamlining reporting and budgeting processes, the university significantly improved departmental planning and accountability. Similarly, the University of Michigan used BI to analyze enrollment trends, allowing them to adjust course scheduling based on actual student demand—demonstrating how BI supports better academic planning and resource utilization.

Harvard University provides a strong example of BI use in advancement and fundraising. With analytics-driven insights, they were able to track donor engagement and fine-tune fundraising strategies to increase philanthropic contributions. Meanwhile, the University of Texas at Austin focused its BI efforts on the research domain, where tracking grants and optimizing proposal submissions enhanced both compliance and research output.

Institutions such as MIT and University of Oxford used BI to support student success and recruitment, respectively. MIT's use of BI to predict academic risk factors enabled targeted interventions, while Oxford improved its marketing and outreach strategies through recruitment data analytics. Lastly, the University of Cambridge applied BI at the faculty and research level, using dashboards to monitor performance metrics and optimize resource allocation, reinforcing their commitment to research excellence.

The table underscores the diverse yet impactful applications of BI across leading higher education institutions. Each university adapted BI tools to fit their strategic priorities—whether in finance, academics, fundraising, research, or recruitment. Common benefits observed include improved decision-making, enhanced operational efficiency, better student outcomes, and increased stakeholder engagement.

These success stories illustrate that when implemented effectively, BI can drive meaningful transformation in higher education by making data accessible,

**Table 1.1** BI in higher education institutions

| No | University | Business intelligence application | Outcome/impact | Reference |
|---|---|---|---|---|
| 1 | University of California, Berkeley | Implemented a BI solution to streamline financial reporting, improve budget planning, and enhance data-driven decision-making across departments | Increased transparency in budgeting, faster financial reporting, and improved departmental planning | UC Berkeley Financial Systems |
| 2 | University of Michigan | Used BI tools to analyze enrollment data, identify course demand trends, and optimize scheduling to better utilize resources | Enhanced course availability, better alignment with student needs, and more efficient resource use | University of Michigan |
| 3 | Harvard University | Leveraged BI to analyze fundraising efforts, track donor contributions, and refine strategies to boost philanthropic support | Higher donor engagement, improved campaign planning, and increased contributions to university programs | Harvard Development |
| 4 | University of Texas at Austin | Adopted BI for analyzing research funding, monitoring grant spending, and improving proposal processes for greater research compliance and output | Greater research productivity, better funding management, and improved compliance with grant conditions | UT Austin Office |
| 5 | Massachusetts Institute of Technology (MIT) | Applied BI to examine student data, determine factors affecting student success, and develop personalized retention strategies | Improved student retention and academic performance through targeted academic support | MIT Institutional |
| 6 | University of Oxford | Used BI analytics on recruitment data to refine outreach strategies and improve marketing efforts to increase enrollment rates | Increased number of high-quality applicants and more effective marketing campaigns | Oxford Undergraduate |
| 7 | University of Cambridge | Deployed BI dashboards to monitor faculty metrics, track research productivity, and support strategic resource allocation | Improved academic performance tracking and strategic investment in faculty and research development | Cambridge Research |

actionable, and aligned with institutional goals. They also show that BI is not a one-size-fits-all solution but a flexible framework that can be tailored to support various facets of academic operations.

## 1.4 Chapter Conclusion

In an era of rapid digital transformation and increasing institutional complexity, Business Intelligence (BI) has emerged as an indispensable tool for higher education institutions striving to remain competitive, responsive, and data-driven. This chapter has explored the strategic value of BI in enhancing decision-making, optimizing resources, improving student outcomes, and supporting compliance and accreditation efforts. By transforming vast volumes of data into actionable insights, BI empowers academic leaders and administrators to align their operational activities with institutional goals, respond swiftly to emerging challenges, and continuously improve performance.

The integration of BI into higher education is not merely a technological upgrade but a fundamental shift in institutional culture. It fosters a proactive rather than reactive approach to management, enabling institutions to move beyond traditional reporting and embrace predictive analytics, performance dashboards, and real-time monitoring. From tracking student progress and refining curriculum offerings to enhancing financial planning and supporting research excellence, BI enables a holistic view of institutional health and sustainability.

Furthermore, real-world case studies from globally renowned universities such as UC Berkeley, MIT, Harvard, and Oxford demonstrate the tangible impact of BI when aligned with institutional priorities. These examples reinforce the notion that successful BI implementation is driven not only by technology but also by leadership commitment, data governance, and a clear understanding of stakeholder needs. As higher education becomes increasingly competitive and student-centered, BI offers the strategic advantage of agility, transparency, and informed planning.

Looking ahead, the role of BI will continue to evolve, particularly with the integration of artificial intelligence, machine learning, and advanced data visualization. Institutions that invest in BI infrastructure and cultivate a data-literate culture will be better positioned to navigate future challenges and capitalize on opportunities. Ultimately, the adoption of BI is not just a matter of efficiency—it is a critical enabler of excellence, innovation, and long-term institutional resilience in the knowledge economy.

# Chapter 2
# Data Governance and Management

## 2.1 Introduction

Effective business intelligence relies heavily on meticulous data governance and management practices. This chapter explores these facets within higher education, considering diverse data sources such as enrolment trends, academic metrics, financial operations, and research. It contextualizes the pivotal role of data, tracing the historical evolution of business intelligence and emphasizing its transformative potential. The chapter underscores the imperative of data governance beyond regulatory compliance, positioning it as crucial for institutional success amid increasing competition and demands for transparency. A concise preview outlines forthcoming exploration of foundational concepts, practical strategies, advanced data management, and the balance between privacy and accessibility.

In the simplest terms, data governance establishes policies and procedures around data, while data management enacts those policies and procedures to compile and use that data for decision-making. To unpack this idea further, it helps to understand what each of these concepts is to better understand how they operate together in practice.

Data governance is a key component of data management—the practice of managing how the data that is being managed is processed through the organization. Data governance helps answer questions like:

- Who has ownership of the data?
- Who can access what data?
- What security measures are in place to protect data and privacy?
- How much of our data is compliant with new regulations?
- Which data sources are approved to use?

Data management is the creation and implementation of architectures, policies, and procedures that manage the full data lifecycle needs of an organization.



A. A. Aziz et al., *Business Intelligence for Higher Education*,
https://doi.org/10.1007/978-3-032-05361-9_2

Having these policies and procedures in place is critical to analyse complex, big data. When data is treated as an important company asset, it needs to be managed as such. Data management includes several different types of data projects, one of which is data governance. We'll quickly review the other common elements of data management before focusing on how data governance and data management work together.

Regarding the education environment, data governance and management including identifying stakeholders of data (e.g. academician, student, university top management) and the sources systems (e.g. Learning Management System, Academic System, HR system) involves building data infrastructure. It is an important process to ensure all the data needed is extracted from the sources. Also, analysis helps to improve decision making especially in the teaching and learning process.

## 2.2 Data Quality (DQ)

Effective decision-making by management is crucial for a company's survival in a competitive market. As a result, the quality of data provided by a data warehouse (DW) becomes essential for organizations seeking to make informed decisions and drive their business forward. DW systems have long captured the interest of both practitioners and researchers, with data quality (DQ) emerging as a critical concern. The success of a DW implementation often hinges on DQ and without it, the investment in such systems can become a waste of resources.

DQ is commonly defined as the ratio of performance to expectations or the societal loss incurred from the moment a product is delivered. In simpler terms, data quality refers to whether the data is "fit for use." Some definitions also emphasize the "freshness" of data as a key measure of quality, as data consumers often prioritize receiving timely and up-to-date information. However, ensuring a high level of DQ in DW projects is one of the most costly and time-consuming challenges organizations face.

A study conducted by Bouzeghoub & Kedad (2002), defines the nature of source data in three main categories. Table 2.1 illustrated the category will help to determine whether the data is fresh or not.

In the early days of DW, one of the biggest challenges was gathering data from disparate distributed systems and organizing it to support an analytic framework. Mapping various data from different source systems into a unified format that everyone could agree on was a complex and tedious task. This time-consuming process had a significant impact on the overall architecture of the DW system. A simple example is the process of address matching, where each source system had its own definitions, constraints, and structured formats for address attributes. Consolidating these different formats into a single address structure before integrating them into the DW was a particularly challenging task.

**Table 2.1** Category of data

| Category | Definition | Examples | Change frequency | Implication on data freshness |
|---|---|---|---|---|
| Stable data | Data that is highly unlikely to change over time | – University names<br>– Person names<br>– Postal codes<br>– Student results<br>– Country names | Rare or Never | High freshness longevity; infrequent updates required |
| Long-term changing data | Data that changes slowly or periodically over long durations | – Student addresses<br>– National currencies<br>– Lists of academic programs offered by universities | Infrequent (e.g., months/ years) | Moderate freshness longevity; periodic updates needed |
| Frequently-changing data | Data that changes frequently, either at defined intervals or randomly | – Real-time traffic information<br>– Temperature sensor readings<br>– Sales quantities<br>– Restaurant menus (daily)<br>– Account balances (random) | High (e.g., hourly/daily/ random) | Low freshness longevity; continuous or scheduled updates necessary for accuracy |

Several factors contribute to the complexity of the DQ process:

1. Different model definitions and representations for common business objects
   Each OLTP system often has isolated development processes for underlying data models, records, structures, and data element formats. For example, the definition and structure of an attribute like "VENDOR" may vary across different OLTP systems.
2. Unstructured and complex data
   Some source systems store data in unstructured formats, which can be essential for analytical processes. These unstructured formats, such as manually entered text files, pose additional challenges during integration.
3. Measuring synchronization and consistency
   Synchronization is determined by the degree to which applications require a consistent view of data. Key dimensions to consider include timeliness, currency, latency, consistency, and the deterministic nature of data access. Ensuring these factors align across systems is crucial for maintaining DQ.

## 2.3 Measuring DQ

DQ can be assessed from two distinct perspectives: the quality of design and the quality of conformance. The quality of design refers to how well data structures, standards, and processes are initially defined to meet intended requirements. In contrast, the quality of conformance evaluates how accurately and consistently data adheres to these predefined standards in real-world applications.

1. Quality of design

   The quality of design is primarily assessed from a technical perspective, focusing on the structural integrity of the data. This involves evaluating the data schema, requiring data warehouse (DW) developers to conduct an in-depth analysis of data modeling, functional specifications, and technical requirements. Each attribute and table must be clearly defined to ensure consistency and reliability. Additionally, the usefulness of the data must be considered. Business stakeholders play a crucial role in identifying relevant data, while IT professionals must determine its sources and ensure proper integration.
2. Quality of Conformance

   The quality of conformance relies on both the timeliness and plausibility of data. In a data DW system, data timeliness is largely dependent on the ETL process. The volume of data that needs to be loaded and transformed directly impacts the time required to generate reports from the DW. To ensure reliability, data must be accurate, promptly available, and transparent. Additionally, data completeness is closely linked to the efficiency of the ETL process. As the demand for more complete and high-quality data increases, the complexity of the ETL process also grows, which in turn affects overall timeliness.

## 2.4 Data Quality Process

The DQ process always refers to the data preprocessing stage. Data preprocessing, a component of data preparation, describes any type of processing performed on raw data to prepare it for another data processing procedure. It has traditionally been an important preliminary step for the data mining process. More recently, data preprocessing techniques have been adapted for training machine learning models and AI models and for running inferences against them.

Data preprocessing transforms the data into a format that is more easily and effectively processed in data mining, machine learning and other data science tasks. The techniques are generally used at the earliest stages of the machine learning and AI development pipeline to ensure accurate results as shown in Fig. 2.1.

DQ plays a key role in earlier stages of machine learning and AI application development, as noted earlier. In an AI context, data preprocessing is used to improve the way data is cleansed, transformed and structured to improve the accuracy of a new model, while reducing the amount of compute required. A good data preprocessing pipeline can create reusable components that make it easier to test out various ideas for streamlining business processes or improving customer satisfaction. For example, preprocessing can improve the way data is organized for a recommendation engine by improving the age ranges used for categorizing customers.

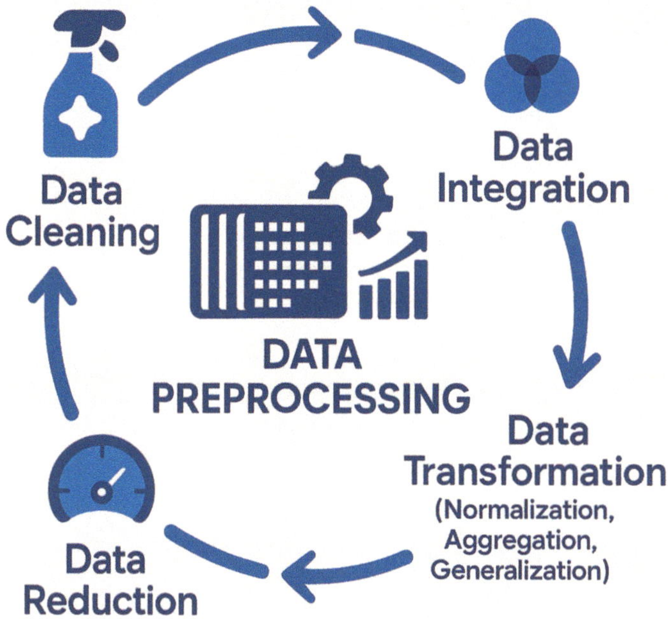


**Fig. 2.1** Data preprocessing process

Preprocessing can also simplify the work of creating and modifying data for more accurate and targeted business intelligence insights. For example, students' records may exist from various systems in educational context (e.g. academic systems, Learning Management System (LMS), sport performance system) may exhibit different behaviors across the systems. Preprocessing the data into the appropriate forms could help BI teams weave these insights into BI dashboards.

Real-world data is messy and is often created, processed and stored by a variety of humans, business processes and applications. As a result, a data set may be missing individual fields, contain manual input errors, or have duplicate data or different names to describe the same thing. Humans can often identify and rectify these problems in the data they use in the line of business, The steps used in data preprocessing depicted in the Fig. 2.2.

1. Data profiling.

   Data profiling constitutes the critical initial phase in data preprocessing. This exploratory step involves an in-depth examination, analysis, and synthesis of metadata from various data sources. The objective is to generate descriptive statistics and detailed summaries of data sets, highlighting anomalies, inconsistencies, and distinctive characteristics. Data scientists utilize profiling to establish a comprehensive understanding of the data's structural, semantic, and quality

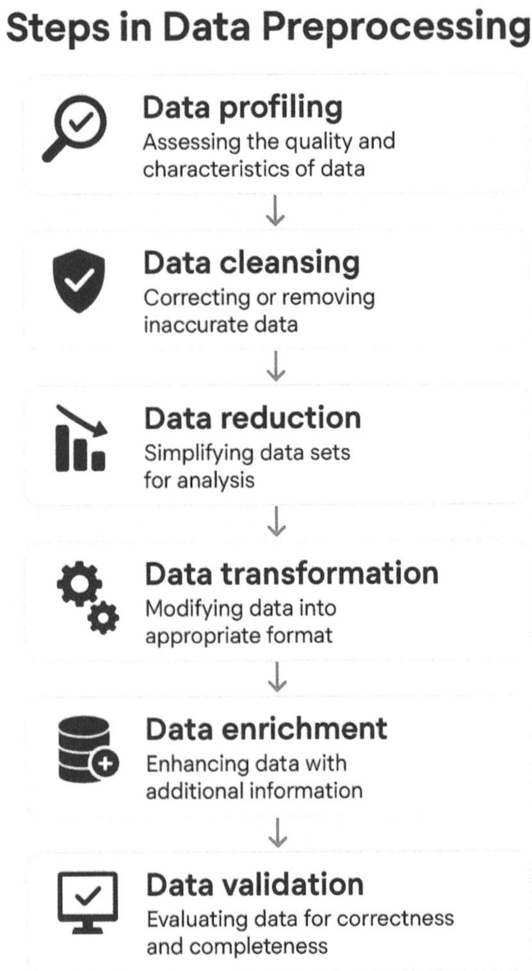


**Fig. 2.2** Steps in data preprocessing

dimensions. Typical activities within data profiling include frequency distribution analysis, detection of missing values, duplicate records identification, uniqueness assessment, and data type validation. Profiling supports hypothesis formation regarding potential feature relevance and lays the groundwork for subsequent preprocessing actions. Furthermore, it informs strategic decisions in data warehouse design and clarifies the discrepancies between actual data structures and stakeholders' perceptions or expectations of their operational data.

2. Data cleansing.

   Following profiling, data cleansing systematically addresses quality issues uncovered in the initial analysis. This critical phase targets correcting errors, handling inconsistencies, and filling gaps to ensure data integrity, reliability, and completeness. Common tasks involve eliminating incorrect or corrupted records, imputing missing values using statistical or machine-learning approaches, correcting inaccurate entries through normalization, and removing or merging duplicate records. Cleansing ensures that the processed data aligns closely with the requirements of subsequent analytical tasks, significantly improving accuracy and reducing computational overhead. Given the importance of accurate modeling outcomes, cleansing directly impacts the reliability and robustness of AI and machine learning predictions.

3. Data reduction.

   Data reduction streamlines complex, voluminous datasets into manageable forms without significantly sacrificing the analytical value of the information. This step mitigates the problems of redundancy, irrelevance, and dimensional complexity that frequently characterize raw datasets. Techniques employed include dimensionality reduction (e.g., Principal Component Analysis (PCA), Independent Component Analysis (ICA)), feature selection methods (such as information gain, mutual information, and recursive feature elimination), and instance reduction strategies (e.g., clustering or sampling). The ultimate aim is to create a concise representation that retains essential characteristics pertinent to the predictive or analytical task, thus optimizing computational efficiency, minimizing storage costs, and enhancing model performance.

4. Data transformation.

   The transformation stage focuses on restructuring and modifying data to enhance its utility for specific analytical tasks, model development, and performance optimization. Data transformation methods may include normalization and scaling (standardization or min-max scaling), discretization (converting continuous variables into categorical bins), encoding categorical variables (one-hot encoding, label encoding), aggregation (combining related variables into composite indicators), and converting unstructured data (e.g., text, images) into structured, numerical formats. These transformations help harmonize datasets from heterogeneous sources, establish consistency across variables, and generate more discriminative features, which significantly improve the predictive power and interpretability of machine learning and AI models.

5. Data enrichment.

   Data enrichment enhances original datasets by augmenting them with additional contextual information, derived features, or external sources, thereby increasing their analytical value. This process involves applying sophisticated feature engineering methods—leveraging domain expertise and computational techniques—to create novel attributes that better represent underlying patterns or relationships. For instance, enrichment may include appending demographic data, geolocation-based insights, external benchmarks, or user-defined adjustable metrics to improve decision-making capabilities. Additionally, enrichment can incorporate standardization practices not initially present in operational systems, aligning data more closely with analytical goals. The enriched dataset thus facilitates deeper insights, enhanced business intelligence reporting, and superior predictive modeling performance.

6. Data validation.

   The validation stage critically assesses the processed dataset's suitability and effectiveness for the intended analytical or machine-learning task. Typically, this step involves partitioning the dataset into distinct subsets: a training set for model development and a separate test set for evaluating model generalization and predictive robustness. Validation metrics, such as accuracy, precision, recall, F1-score, and AUC-ROC, are computed to objectively measure the model's performance and identify potential deficiencies in data preprocessing methodologies, including cleansing and transformation techniques. Rigorous validation enables data scientists to iteratively refine preprocessing methods and feature engineering hypotheses. Upon achieving satisfactory validation outcomes, the preprocessing pipeline is documented and escalated for production implementation, usually overseen by data engineers, who ensure scalability, efficiency, and reproducibility of the developed pipeline.

## 2.5 Chapter Conclusion

Effective business intelligence is intrinsically linked to robust data governance and management practices, particularly in the context of higher education. This chapter has explored these critical aspects by examining diverse data sources such as enrollment patterns, academic performance metrics, financial records, and research outputs. By tracing the evolution of business intelligence, we have highlighted the transformative potential of data-driven decision-making and underscored the increasing importance of transparency and compliance in data governance.

At its core, data governance establishes the policies and procedures necessary for ensuring data integrity, security, and accessibility, while data management operationalizes these policies to ensure data is efficiently processed, stored, and utilized. Within educational institutions, data governance involves defining ownership, regulating access, ensuring compliance with evolving regulations, and maintaining data security measures. Concurrently, data management ensures that institutional data infrastructures integrate multiple source systems—such as Learning Management Systems (LMS), Academic Systems, and Human Resources (HR) platforms—into a cohesive framework that facilitates informed decision-making.

A key focus of this chapter has been on data quality (DQ), which is fundamental for making reliable decisions. Poor data quality in data warehousing (DW) systems can result in flawed insights, rendering significant investments in analytics ineffective. We have classified data based on its stability—ranging from stable data (e.g., university names) to frequently changing data (e.g., student enrollments or financial transactions). This classification aids in assessing data freshness and ensuring that decision-makers rely on timely and accurate information.

The chapter has also outlined the complexities of ensuring high data quality, addressing challenges such as disparate data definitions, unstructured formats, and synchronization issues across multiple systems. We examined the dual perspectives of data quality—design quality (ensuring well-structured data schemas and integration processes) and conformance quality (measuring how well data adheres to these predefined standards). The effectiveness of a data warehouse is heavily dependent on its Extract, Transform, and Load (ETL) processes, which influence data completeness, timeliness, and reliability.

Finally, we explored the data quality process within data preprocessing, a critical step in preparing data for machine learning and artificial intelligence applications. Techniques such as data profiling, cleansing, transformation, enrichment, and validation ensure that raw data is refined into a format suitable for analysis and decision-making. These processes are particularly crucial in higher education, where data from multiple systems must be integrated to enhance business intelligence insights, improve academic performance tracking, and streamline administrative processes.

# Chapter 3
# BI Tools and Technologies for Higher Education

## 3.1 Introduction

Business intelligence (BI) tools provide intuitive insights into raw data extracted from an integrated data warehouse (DW), offering a broad spectrum of analytical capabilities. These tools transform raw data into meaningful information and, subsequently, into actionable knowledge, which is presented to business managers through visually appealing interfaces such as graphs, charts, pie charts, tables, geospatial maps, and other statistical diagrams. Beyond data visualization, BI tools serve as essential intermediaries between raw data and informed decision-making, incorporating advanced analytics, reporting, and data integration functionalities to form the backbone of intelligent decision support systems.

While BI has been defined in various ways, all interpretations align with its core principles. It is a computer-based system designed for in-depth business data analysis, capable of identifying patterns, drilling through data, making predictions, and cross-referencing information from multiple sources. BI can also be conceptualized as a centralized hub of fact-based decision support systems, integrating diverse tools with unique architectures, methodologies, and databases. These components work collectively to provide critical insights, empowering business owners to make well-informed, strategic decisions.

Not all benefits brought by BI to numerous industrial sectors can be seen at first sight. Experts generally agree that BI gives companies' certain benefits that are difficult to define precisely because of their indirect and delayed effort on business success while other benefits are unpredictable and can only be seen after a certain period of using BI. One of the most key benefits of BI is its ability to improve support for decision making. Other benefits that BI aims to create are increase in efficiency and effectiveness of an organisation; enable users to quickly understand complex data; assist in effectively achieving business goals; enable a faster flow and easier access to information within an organisation; provides faster and more



A. A. Aziz et al., *Business Intelligence for Higher Education*,
https://doi.org/10.1007/978-3-032-05361-9_3

accurate reporting; improves customer satisfaction; increases revenues, profit and market share of an organisation.

## 3.2 Components and Techniques of BI Tools

Business Intelligence (BI) systems are built using a suite of tools, each designed with specific functionalities and capabilities. Among these, data warehouses serve as the foundation of BI and are considered the most fundamental component. As a result, organizations are investing significant resources in data collection, extraction, and analytical technologies. The integration of data warehousing and BI has significantly improved business processes, acting as a crucial driver for sustained growth in business value and performance.

BI tools encompass a range of technologies that convert vast amounts of data into meaningful and actionable insights through real-time analysis. This enables business managers to identify trends, make informed decisions, and uncover new opportunities. These tools facilitate a value chain of processes that leverage diverse technologies, architectures, techniques, and functionalities. Key technologies and components commonly found in a BI platform include:

### *3.2.1 Data Integration*

Data integration tools are a critical component in any business intelligence system. It involves integrating data from different data sources (ERP Systems, Management Information System, Applications, and Flat-files) into a single repository (Data warehouse). In business intelligence, structured, semi-structured, and unstructured data can be integrated under a single repository of an up-to-date version of all data. Data integration tools use the ETL to store, manage and process large volumes of data. Data integrated through this model can be easily manipulated, utilized, queried using analytical processes, and retrieved.

With the emergence of operational BI, it has become imperative to adopt the new generation of data integration architecture that can plug-in several requirements needed by a BI system. These requirements include the support for a large number of data mart connections; fast refresh cycles; more complex reporting and analytic tools; consistent connectivity; support for diverse data types and sources.

Figure 3.1 shows a basic architecture, and processes carried out using data integration tools on a BI platform. Some of the processes include:

**Metadata** Typically defined as data about data. Metadata is designed for different tasks ranging from content filtering, information management, archiving, and so much more. Metadata is an operation carried out in data integration to provide description on data condition, origin, and other characteristics of data.

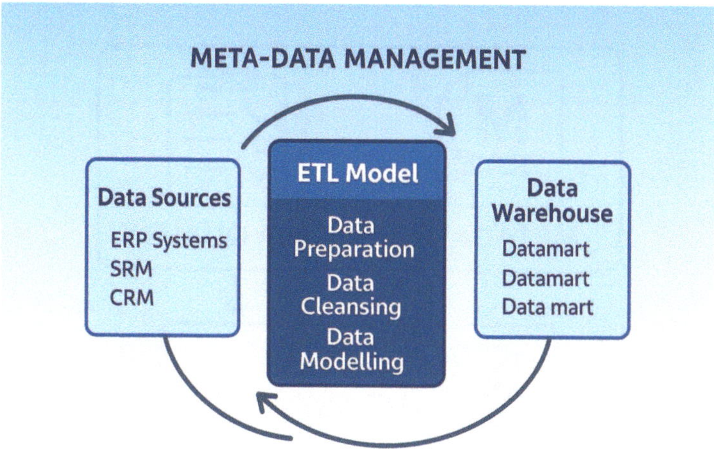


**Fig. 3.1** Data integration architecture

**Data Quality** Set to ensure conformity of data values to business requirements and acceptance criteria. Data workflow and collaboration are required capabilities in Data Integration processes. This capability enables BI users to integrate BI results within the context of a specific business process and to discuss information via public folder or discussion thread (Fig. 3.2).

### 3.2.2 *Data Warehousing*

The concept of DW emerged in the late 1980s with the introduction of the term "Business Data Warehousing". It was developed in response to the growing need for seamless access to consolidated, high-quality organizational data to support strategic decision-making. DW is characterized as a subject-oriented, integrated, time-variant, and non-volatile repository of data designed to aid managerial decision-making processes.

Figure 3.3 above shows comprehensive concepts of a DW where data can be collated from different data sources, systems, or applications and harmonized into a single up-to-date repository.

### 3.2.3 *Analytics*

Analytics plays a crucial role in identifying, developing, and structuring data patterns into valuable insights. It involves interpreting large volumes of data and theoretical frameworks, transforming them into meaningful and actionable information

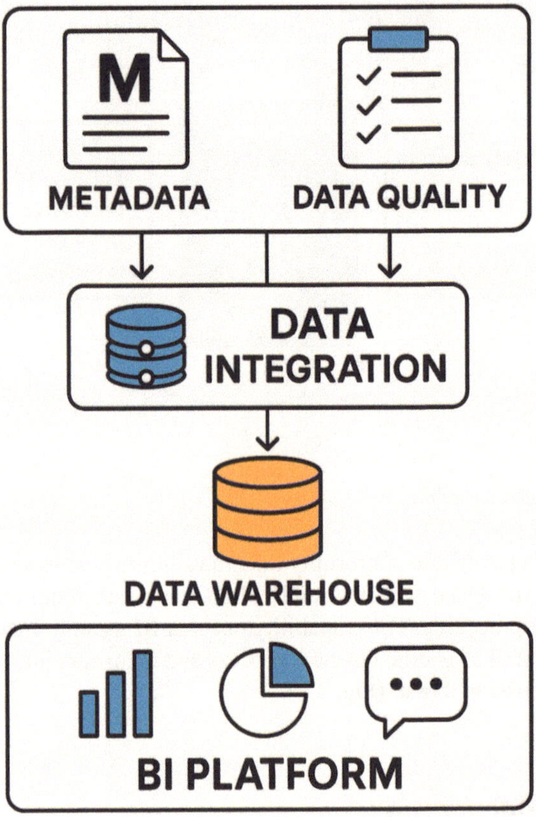


**Fig. 3.2** Metadata and data quality

for business purposes. Analytical processes include responding to ad-hoc queries, forecasting trends, conducting real-time analysis, generating reports, and performing operations such as slicing-and-dicing and drill-down exploration. While various technologies are used for business intelligence (BI) analysis, Online Analytical Processing (OLAP) tools and data visualization are considered the most effective components for comprehensive analysis. Analytics are what translate data into meaningful information. Data are analysed with extremely fast queries and calculation performance using OLAP capabilities to slice and dice through data. Some of the processes of analytics include:

**Data Mining** Data mining is the process of analyzing vast amounts of data to uncover hidden patterns, relationships, and meaningful insights that can aid in decision-making. It involves extracting useful information from large datasets by identifying trends, correlations, and anomalies. The process relies on various advanced technologies, including artificial intelligence (AI), machine learning

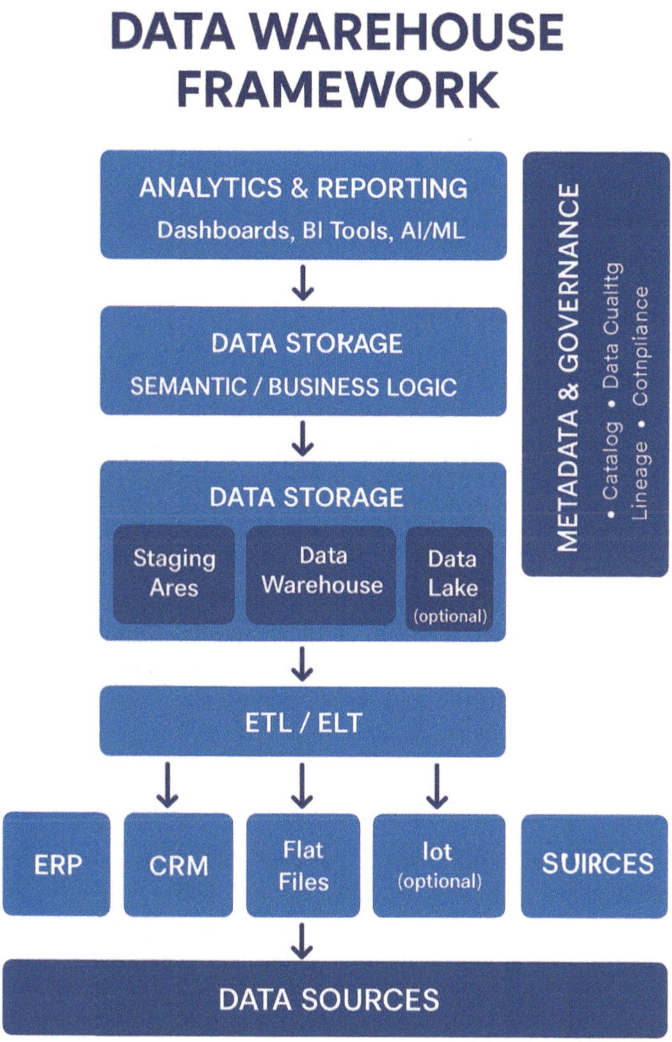


**Fig. 3.3** Concept of data warehouse

(ML), statistical modeling, and database management techniques, to classify, cluster, associate, and predict outcomes based on historical data.

At its core, data mining encompasses several key techniques:

- **Classification:** Assigning predefined labels or categories to data based on specific attributes. For example, classifying customer transactions as "fraudulent" or "legitimate."

- **Clustering:** Grouping similar data points together without predefined categories, helping to identify natural structures within data, such as customer segmentation in marketing.
- **Association Rule Mining:** Detecting relationships between different variables in a dataset, commonly used in market basket analysis to determine purchasing behaviors.
- **Prediction & Forecasting:** Using historical data to make informed predictions about future trends, such as sales forecasting or risk assessment

#### 3.2.3.1 Educational Data Mining

Educational Data Mining (EDM) is the process of applying data mining techniques to analyse data generated within educational environments to improve learning outcomes, teaching practices, and institutional efficiency. By examining data from sources such as student performance records, learning management systems, and online learning platforms, EDM helps identify patterns and trends that can be used to personalize learning, predict student success, improve curriculum design, and optimize resource planning. For example, institutions can use EDM to detect students at risk of dropping out, enabling early interventions, or to evaluate the effectiveness of course content. Through its predictive capabilities, EDM supports data-driven decision-making, fostering a more effective, personalized, and adaptive educational experience for both students and educators.

#### 3.2.3.2 Educational Intelligence

Educational Intelligence (EI) refers to the integration of advanced data analytics, artificial intelligence (AI), and machine learning (ML) techniques to enhance decision-making, optimize educational processes, and improve outcomes for both students and institutions. As educational systems become more data-rich, EI plays a crucial role in transforming this data into actionable insights, supporting personalized learning, efficient resource management, and strategic planning. EI concept was first proposed by Aziz et al. (Chen et al., 2012), which includes three main features: data warehouse which is designed for HEIs and the implement of EDM along with the OLAP engine for educational data reporting; the ability to perform multiple analytic processes of descriptive analysis and predictive analysis; a friendly reporting user interface.

**Knowledge Management** This is the core engine that performs various jobs, aiding the non-trivial process of identifying potentially useful and ultimately understandable patterns in data. It uses different steps, which include data projection, data reduction and data acquisition.

### 3.2.4 Information Presentation

Information is presented using interactive data Visualization process which makes discovered knowledge easily understood using charts, plots, histograms, and other visual means. The reporting system used in information presentation uses customized and flexible processes generated from multidimensional and relational data sources. Some key features of information presentation include:

**Data Visualization** This is a general term used to describe any technology that allows users to understand the information and significance of any volume of data. Today's data visualization tools display data in a more sophisticated way such as infographics, geographical maps, gauges, detailed bar and pie charts. Most BI now embeds data visualization tools into their products to enable users to manipulate and drill into data for querying and analysis.

**Dashboard** A BI dashboard is referred to as a graphical interface that displays the current status of key performance indicators, metrics, and statistics for a particular enterprise. Dashboards are used to consolidate and arrange numbers, performance scorecards, and metrics on a single display screen. It is sometimes tailored for a specific role; however, its major feature is its ability to pull real-time data from multiple data sources. Figure 3.4 below shows a sample dashboard of a BI platform.

### 3.2.5 Online Analytical Processing (OLAP)

Online Analytical Processing (OLAP) is a computer-based technique used to analyze data for extracting meaningful insights. It enables users to perform real-time data analysis and is often referred to as Multidimensional Analysis (MDA). OLAP provides superior performance compared to traditional Online Transaction Processing (OLTP) systems by precomputing and summarizing expected queries into multidimensional views before execution. This approach enhances efficiency and supports complex analytical operations and data visualization. OLAP is commonly implemented within data warehouses or data marts to facilitate advanced enterprise intelligence solutions.

OLAP plays a crucial role in various business processes, including strategic planning, forecasting, budgeting, and decision-making. It assists in constructing business models that enable users to derive insights and make informed decisions rapidly. Due to its analytical capabilities, OLAP serves as the foundation for many business intelligence applications. OLAP systems are primarily categorized into three types as depicted in Fig. 3.5.

- **Multidimensional OLAP (MOLAP):** Stores data in a multidimensional cube format, optimizing query performance through pre-aggregated data.

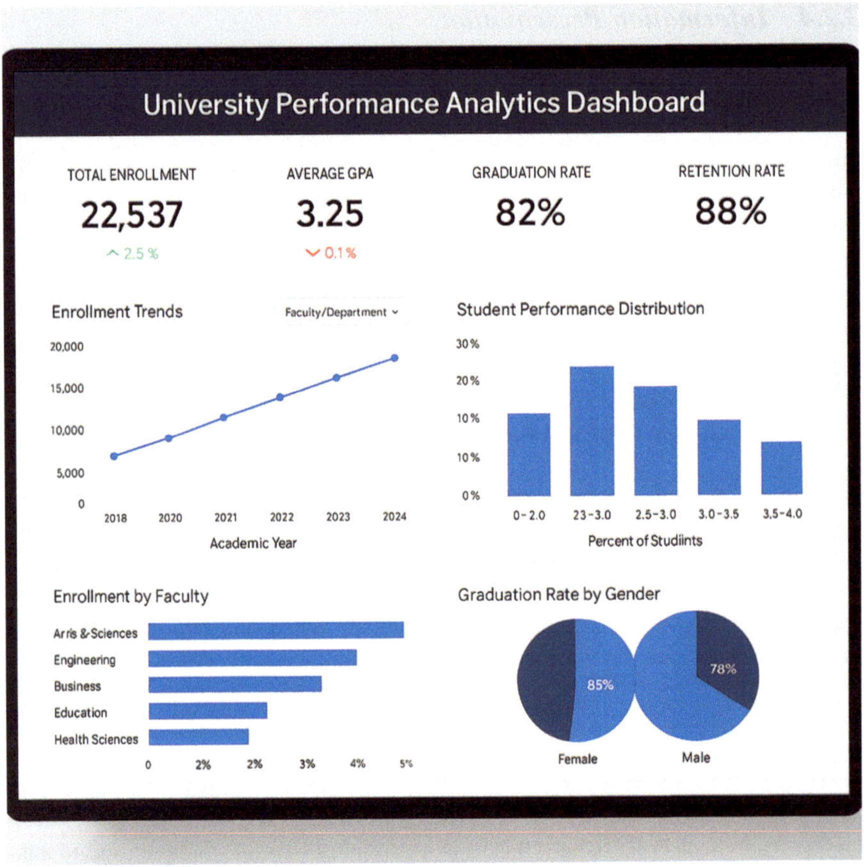


**Fig. 3.4** A sample dashboard for university performance analytics

- **Relational OLAP (ROLAP):** Uses relational databases to store and query multidimensional data dynamically, without pre-aggregation.
- **Hybrid OLAP (HOLAP):** A combination of MOLAP and ROLAP, leveraging the strengths of both for improved flexibility and performance.

Data in OLAP systems is typically structured using either a star schema or a snowflake schema within a relational data warehouse or a specialized data management system. The fact table holds measurable business metrics (measures), while dimension tables provide contextual attributes for analysis. These structured representations allow organizations to perform in-depth analytical queries efficiently, supporting data-driven decision-making across industries.

Figure 3.6 provides an OLAP design framework. This design framework usually has multiple dimensions for high-speed performance queries. Some of the operations that can be carried out using OLAP are illustrates in Table 3.1.

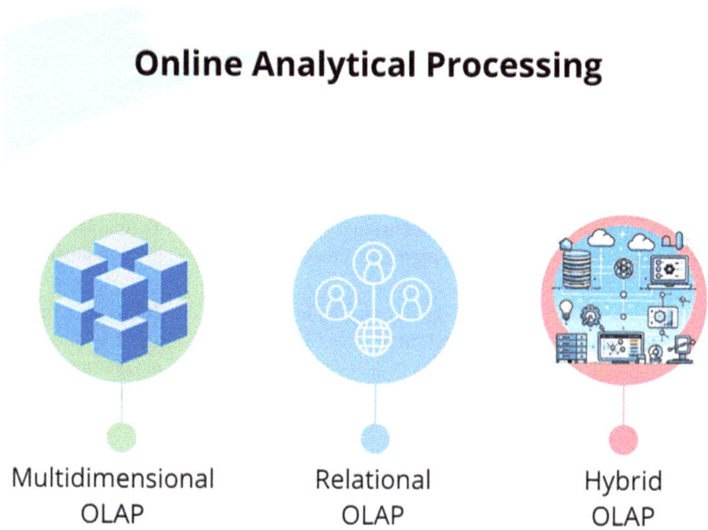


**Fig. 3.5** Types of categories in OLAP

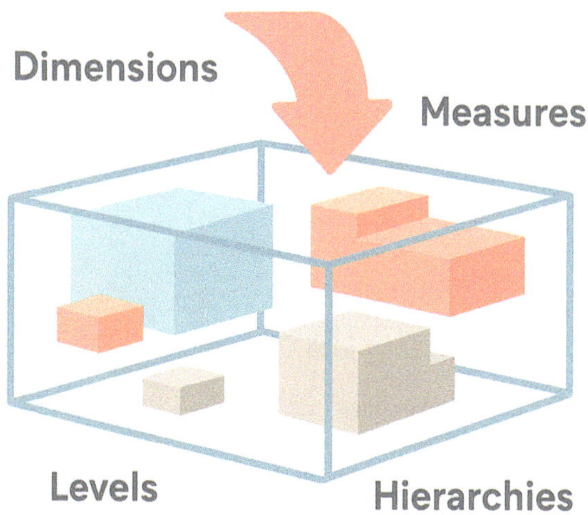


**Fig. 3.6** OLAP analytical design framework

**Table 3.1** OLAP operation description

| OLAP operation | Description | Purpose |
|---|---|---|
| Slicing and dicing | Slicing selects a rectangular subset of the data cube by fixing a value in one dimension, reducing dimensionality. Dicing selects specific values across multiple dimensions | To view specific sub-cubes of interest from the data cube |
| Roll-up | Aggregates data along a dimension by summarizing it (e.g., totals, averages) using hierarchical levels or predefined formulas | To analyse data at a higher level of abstraction |
| Drill up/down | Allows users to explore data at varying levels of granularity—from general summaries (drill-up) to detailed views (drill-down) | To perform multi-level analysis of data by navigating through hierarchies |

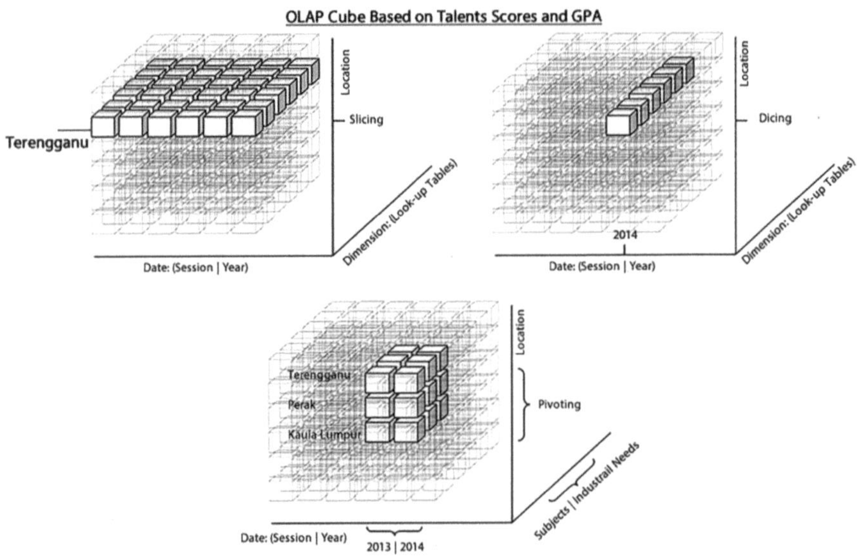


**Fig. 3.7** OLAP slicing, dicing and pivoting

Figure 3.7 above illustrates how an OLAP cube operates slicing, dicing and pivoting operations. Each operation gives a different perspective on how a data is analysed and presented.

## 3.3 Categories of BI Platforms

Business Intelligence (BI) platforms can be broadly categorized into two main types: Open Source BI and Commercial BI. Each category offers a comprehensive suite of tools designed to facilitate data integration, analytics, reporting, and visualization—core functionalities essential to any BI system.

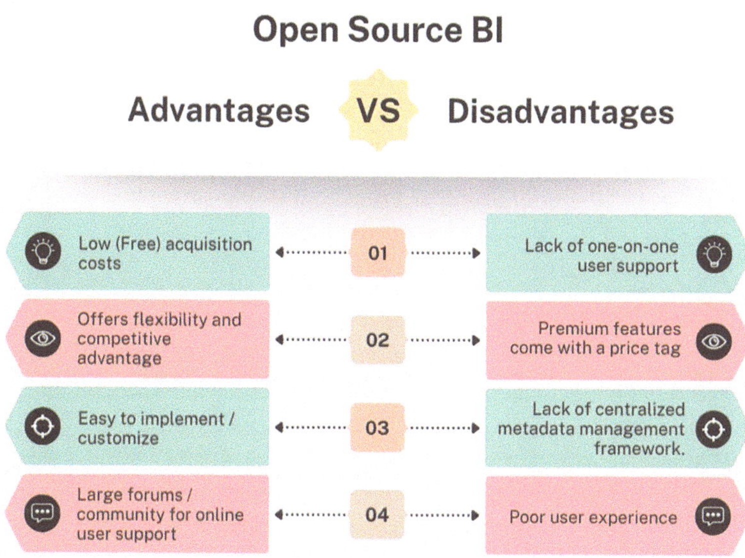


**Fig. 3.8** Advantages and disadvantages in Open-source BI

**Open Source BI platforms** are freely available and often supported by a community of developers who continuously enhance their features, security, and compatibility. These platforms provide businesses with a cost-effective alternative to proprietary solutions while allowing for greater customization and flexibility. Organizations leveraging open-source BI tools can modify and extend the software to meet their specific analytical and reporting needs. However, they may require additional technical expertise for deployment, maintenance, and optimization.

**Commercial BI platforms**, on the other hand, are proprietary solutions developed by technology vendors that provide enterprise-grade support, security, and advanced functionalities. These platforms often include integrated features such as artificial intelligence-driven analytics, machine learning models, and seamless cloud-based deployment. Commercial BI solutions are typically designed to be user-friendly, reducing the need for extensive technical expertise while offering robust customer support and regular updates.

Despite these fundamental differences, all BI platforms aim to transform raw data into actionable insights. Each platform differentiates itself in the market through unique value propositions, strategic branding, and proprietary features tailored to specific business needs, as illustrated in Figs. 3.7, 3.8 and 3.9.

Table 3.2 lists of top BI tools with the key features and enterprise customers.

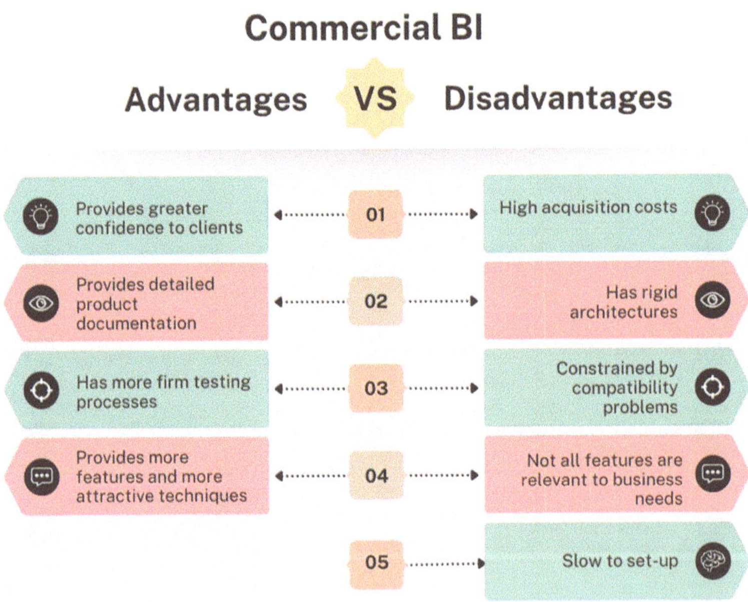


**Fig. 3.9** Advantages and disadvantages in Commercial BI

## 3.4 Applying BI tools in Higher Education

BI is increasingly transforming the higher education sector, helping institutions optimize their operations, enhance student outcomes, and make data-driven strategic decisions. Through BI tools, universities can collect, analyze, and visualize data from different systems—such as admissions, financial aid, student performance, and alumni relations—turning raw data into actionable insights.

For example, the use of analytics at the University of Alabama whereby the university implemented a BI system to help monitor student performance and retention. By analyzing data from course grades, attendance records, and student engagement on online platforms, the university was able to identify students who were at risk of dropping out early in the semester. This proactive use of data allowed academic advisors and faculty to intervene by providing additional support or resources, leading to improved student retention and graduation rates.

Similarly, Texas A&M University has employed BI tools to enhance operational efficiency. The university uses data analytics to track class enrollments, faculty workloads, and facility usage, enabling administrators to better manage classroom assignments, reduce course bottlenecks, and optimize resource allocation. This not only improves the institution's capacity to serve students but also results in cost savings by ensuring more effective use of campus resources.

**Table 3.2** Top list of BI tools

| BI tool | Type | Key features | Enterprise customers |
|---|---|---|---|
| Microsoft Power BI | Commercial/ Cloud | Self-service BI, interactive dashboards, data visualization, AI features, integration with Microsoft stack | Heathrow Airport, Nestlé, Rolls-Royce, BP, Adobe |
| Tableau | Commercial/ Cloud | Visual analytics, drag-and-drop dashboarding, advanced analytics, big data support | Verizon, JPMorgan Chase, Lufthansa, Pfizer, LinkedIn |
| Qlik Sense | Commercial/ Cloud | Associative analytics engine, self-service, real-time data exploration, in-memory processing | Cisco, Samsung, NHS, DocuSign |
| SAP BusinessObjects | Commercial | Enterprise reporting, ad hoc analysis, data discovery, integration with SAP ERP | Shell, Coca-Cola Hellenic, T-Mobile, Citrix |
| IBM Cognos Analytics | Commercial/ Cloud | Automated data preparation, AI-driven insights, reporting, enterprise scalability | Honda, Amtrak, Tupperware, Ricoh |
| Oracle Analytics Cloud (OAC) | Commercial/ Cloud | Data preparation, embedded machine learning, natural language queries, integration with Oracle cloud | Siemens, FedEx, Accenture, Honeywell |
| Google Looker | Commercial/ Cloud | Data modeling, embedded analytics, real-time data exploration, strong cloud integrations | King, The Economist, Sunrun, BuzzFeed |
| MicroStrategy | Commercial/ Cloud | Enterprise analytics, hyperintelligence, mobility, strong security | eBay, McDonald's, Visa, 3 M |
| Sisense | Commercial/ Cloud | Embedded analytics, data unification, scalable architecture, API-first approach | Philips, GE, Nasdaq, Rolls-Royce |
| Domo | Commercial/ Cloud | End-to-end cloud BI, business apps marketplace, real-time dashboards, mobile-first | Unilever, DHL, ESPN, L'Oréal |

In the United Kingdom, the University of Edinburgh integrated BI into its admissions process. By analyzing historical data on applicants, the university was able to predict trends in application volumes and adjust recruitment strategies accordingly. This helped the institution target its outreach efforts more effectively, leading to a more diverse and qualified applicant pool. Additionally, BI helped streamline the processing of applications by highlighting areas of inefficiency, resulting in faster admissions decisions and an improved applicant experience.

BI tools are also proving valuable in financial planning and resource management. For example, the University of Central Florida (UCF) implemented BI to improve its financial aid process. By analyzing data on student demographics, financial aid applications, and academic performance, UCF was able to allocate scholarships and grants more strategically, ensuring that aid was distributed to the students most in need. This not only improved student satisfaction but also helped the university achieve its diversity and inclusion goals.

These real-life examples demonstrate how BI is reshaping higher education by providing institutions with the tools they need to make informed decisions. Whether through student success initiatives, operational improvements, or strategic planning, BI enables universities to respond to challenges proactively and effectively. As higher education continues to evolve, the application of BI will become even more critical in shaping the future of academic institutions, ensuring they remain competitive and focused on student and institutional success.

## 3.5 Chapter Conclusion

Business Intelligence (BI) tools and technologies have become indispensable in the higher education sector, enabling institutions to leverage data-driven insights for informed decision-making, operational efficiency, and improved student outcomes. This chapter has explored the core components of BI, including data integration, data warehousing, analytics, information presentation, and Online Analytical Processing (OLAP), all of which form the foundation of modern BI platforms. By transforming raw data into actionable knowledge, BI tools empower higher education institutions to optimize resources, streamline administrative processes, and enhance the overall learning experience.

A key consideration in selecting a BI solution is the choice between open-source and commercial platforms, each with its advantages and limitations. While open-source BI offers flexibility and cost-effectiveness, commercial BI platforms provide robust support, security, and advanced functionalities. Regardless of the choice, the ultimate goal remains the same: to facilitate intelligent, data-driven decision-making.

The application of BI in higher education has demonstrated tangible benefits, as seen in universities worldwide. Institutions such as the University of Alabama, Texas A&M University, and the University of Edinburgh have successfully harnessed BI tools to improve student retention, optimize operational efficiency, and enhance recruitment strategies. Moreover, financial planning and resource management have been significantly improved through BI, as demonstrated by the University of Central Florida's strategic financial aid allocation.

As data continues to play a critical role in shaping higher education, the adoption of BI will become even more vital. Institutions that effectively integrate BI into their decision-making processes will be better positioned to address challenges such as student retention, resource optimization, and academic performance monitoring. The future of BI in higher education lies in the increasing convergence of artificial intelligence, machine learning, and real-time analytics, which will further enhance predictive capabilities and proactive decision-making.

Ultimately, the implementation of BI tools in higher education represents a transformative shift toward a more data-driven, efficient, and student-centric approach to academic and administrative management. As technology evolves, higher education institutions must continue to embrace BI innovations to remain competitive, responsive, and capable of delivering high-quality education and institutional success.

# Chapter 4
# Building a Data Warehouse for Higher Education

## 4.1 Introduction

Information is globally considered as organizational greatest asset which the success of the organization in gaining competitive edge depends on. As a result of advancement in information technology, storing organizational data or information is no longer a problem irrespective of the nature or magnitude. However, accessing such data easily to harness its value by the organization is increasingly difficult due to the diversity in sources and heterogeneity in formats of the data). Fortunately, the advent of relational databases in the early 1980's provides enhanced access to the vital information buried deep within data. But, that did not suffice, because databases were modeled for smooth transactional processing, and not enhanced to provide sophisticated reporting and analytical services. For this reason, in those days, to provide decision-support or end-user computing services, a new database dedicated to supporting ad hoc end-user query and reporting functions were created. Data will be extracted from organizations online databases which are usually the subset or snapshots of the operational data. Moreover, the extracted data is regularly stored in the newly created database systems which will be available for users equipped with query and reporting tools to access.

## 4.2 Data Warehouse (DW)

In modern enterprise environments, analyzing data can be challenging due to its storage in heterogeneous locations and varied formats across organizational systems. To address this fragmentation and facilitate harmonized enterprise analytics, data warehouses (DWs) have become foundational as integrated, centralized repositories. The evolution of data warehousing as a practice began in the late 1980s, with


A. A. Aziz et al., *Business Intelligence for Higher Education*,
https://doi.org/10.1007/978-3-032-05361-9_4

early foundational work by pioneers such as Bill Inmon and Ralph Kimball. Today, data warehousing continues to be a dynamic and rapidly evolving field, with ongoing innovations in architecture and application (Golfarelli & Rizzi, 2020; Abelló et al., 2023).

Bill Inmon, often referred to as the "Father of Data Warehousing," defined a data warehouse as a subject-oriented, integrated, time-variant, and non-volatile collection of data that supports management's decision-making processes (Inmon, 2005).

- Subject-oriented: Data relevant to specific business domains are consolidated, enabling a comprehensive view of a business area.
- Integrated: Data is standardized and consistent, regardless of its source or original format.
- Time-variant: DWs retain historical data, supporting longitudinal analysis and trend identification, often with explicit time-stamps.
- Non-volatile: Data within a DW is stable and typically read-only, ensuring consistency and optimizing analytical queries.

Building on Inmon's foundation, Ralph Kimball advanced the field through the development of dimensional modeling and advocated for a bottom-up approach, where individual data marts are integrated into a broader warehouse architecture (Kimball & Ross, 2019). Kimball's methodology emphasizes the practical aspects of OLAP (Online Analytical Processing), supporting business users through user-friendly multidimensional data models.

More recently, the field has seen advancements such as cloud data warehousing, real-time analytics, and the integration of data lakes with traditional DWs, reflecting the growing scale and complexity of organizational data needs (Kumar et al., 2021; Abelló et al., 2023). These innovations enable faster, more scalable, and flexible solutions, particularly relevant in the era of big data and artificial intelligence.

In the context of education, data warehouses play a crucial role in integrating disparate data sources, including academic records, learning management systems, and administrative databases—into a unified platform (Suriyapperuma & Kahandawaarachchi, 2022). This integration empowers higher education institutions to streamline operations and generate actionable insights across academic, financial, and operational domains.

A well-structured educational DW enables evidence-based decision-making, supports institutional research, and fosters data-driven improvement initiatives. By providing a consolidated view of institutional data, data warehouses enhance strategic planning and enable a culture of continuous improvement in academic settings. Figure 4.1 presents an example of a contemporary data warehouse framework, illustrating the integration and flow of data from diverse sources to actionable insights.

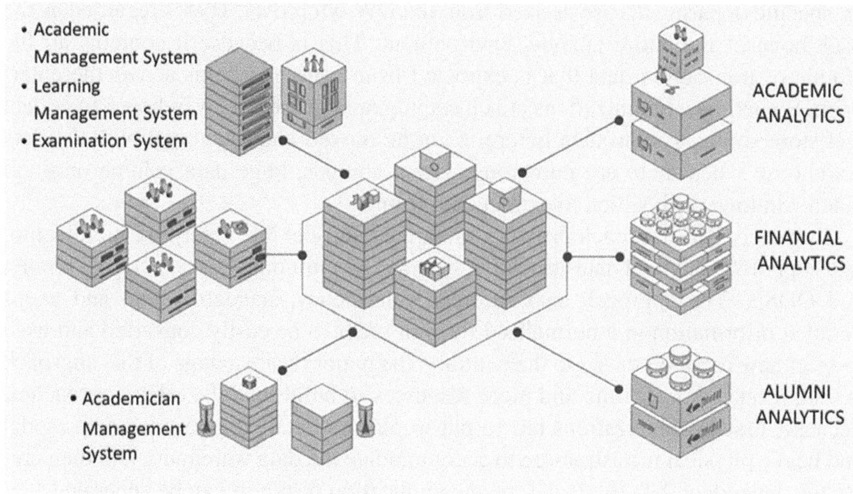


**Fig. 4.1** DW for higher education framework

## *4.2.1 Data Warehouse Approach*

The architecture of DW varies with the building approach used. However, generally DW is made of the following major components.

- Operational/Data source: these are the sources of DW input data, usually records of operational systems that capture business transactions.
- Data staging area: is the part of DW between data sources and data presentation area where the vital extraction, transformation and loading process (ETL) take place. This area does not produce query for business presentation services.
- Storing area: Contain the metadata, physical data and data marts (a subset of data warehouse usually containing data or information of a particular business line that serves as a medium through which users access the data warehouse)
- Data presentation area: this is the part where processed data is organized, stored and made available for direct query by users. These are capabilities that can be provided to business users to enable them exploit the presentation area for analytical decision making such as BI tools

### 4.2.1.1 There are Three Types of DW Approaches

Top-Down Approach

In this approach, the entire DW is firstly built. The DW is built iteratively department by department using a normalized data model to obtain a single version of truth. Subsequently, the dependent dimensional data marts containing data needed by specific departments are derived from the DW. Moreover, DW is regarded as the back-bone of the entire analytic environment. This is because it contains all the atomic or transaction data that is extracted from source systems across the enterprise. Sometimes, organizations attach staging area to the data warehouse to collect and store source system data before it can be moved and integrated with the data warehouse when there are numerous system sources, huge data volume or small batch windows with which to extract data from.

However, This approach provides integrated and flexible enterprise architecture that supports analytical data structures such as Data mining sets, operational reports and ODS's. The approach also enforces consistency, standardization and keeps detailed information in a normalised form in order to be easily converted and used to meet new requirements. On the contrary, the major disadvantage of this approach is that, it takes longer time and more resources to build than the other approaches, because, firstly, organizations has to put in place a detailed enterprise data model and heavy physical infrastructure to accommodate the data warehouse and then create the dependent data marts before any application or report can be generated.

#### Bottom-Up Approach

In this approach, autonomous data marts are initially developed for each department or business line using a multidimensional star schema model with conformed dimensions and facts. The multidimensional model allows data to be stored in a denormalized format, optimizing usability and query performance. Furthermore, the conformed dimensions and facts facilitate the integration of data marts into a centralized database, forming a comprehensive data warehouse. Each data mart supports querying and reporting capabilities, as it contains all necessary user-required data related to that specific business line in both atomic and summary forms for current and future use.

The primary objective of this approach is to deliver business value as efficiently as possible. The incremental development of data marts, with strict adherence to conformed facts and dimensions, enables users to perform cross-mart queries to obtain a unified version of the truth. The bottom-up approach begins by identifying information sources based on user requirements, extracting the relevant data into a staging area, and then processing and transforming it into the desired format. Finally, the information is loaded into a set of interrelated data marts following a multidimensional (star) schema using a dimension bus. Figure 4.2 illustrates the bottom-up (Kimball) architecture.

The bottom-up approach is highly flexible, user-friendly, cost-effective, and faster to implement compared to the top-down approach. It simplifies querying and data retrieval, as users do not need to navigate between multiple data marts. Each data mart contains both atomic and summarized data relevant to its corresponding business line. Additionally, this approach offers short response times and facilitates seamless integration of new data due to its lightweight infrastructure.

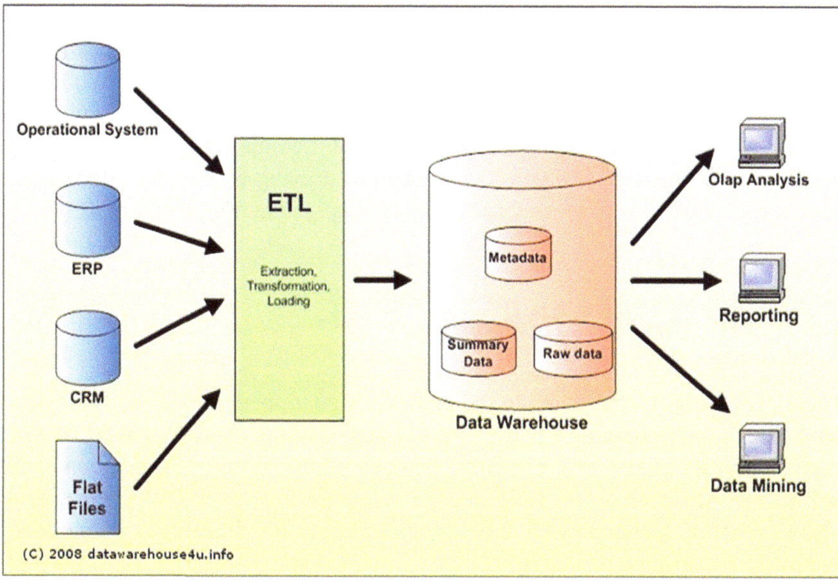


**Fig. 4.2** DW bottom up

However, this approach does not inherently support batch or transaction processing, necessitating additional data structures for operational transaction handling. Furthermore, to achieve integration and maintain a single version of the truth, strict adherence to standardized dimensions and facts is required. This can be particularly challenging in large or decentralized organizations.

## Hybrid Approach

This approach integrates the strengths of both top-down and bottom-up methodologies, prioritizing speed, user-friendliness, and seamless integration with enterprise-wide data management. It begins with a carefully designed enterprise model before developing the initial data mart. In this framework, both the enterprise model and the first few data marts adhere to the third normal form, while the data marts are deployed using a star schema physical model.

The approach relies on Extract, Transform, and Load (ETL) tools to store and manage both local and enterprise models within the data marts while synchronizing any discrepancies between them. This allows local teams to enforce data governance rules derived from the enterprise model without compromising long-term integration. Organizations use ETL tools to populate dimensional data marts with source data at both atomic and summary levels. Once the initial "dependent" data marts are deployed, the organization backfills a data warehouse behind them, transferring atomic data from the data marts to the data warehouse. This process consolidates redundant data feeds, optimizing resource utilization.

However, backfilling the data warehouse can be highly disruptive and may not provide immediate value. Additionally, as this approach is heavily dependent on ETL tools, local teams may easily deviate from standardized processes. While ETL tools have matured over time, ensuring strict adherence to architectural guidelines remains a challenge. Furthermore, users may find it confusing to determine which database to query, as few query tools support retrieving atomic data from a data warehouse while simultaneously accessing summary data from a data mart.

## 4.2.2 DW Modeling Techniques

These are specialized procedures and methods used to model the data in DW. Data modeling is an indispensable part of every data processing operation, thus DW is no exception. Data modeling is important because it provides the visualization of the business world which serves as a guideline to implementation of DW. There are two major modeling techniques for DW, these are Entity Relationship (ER) modeling and multidimensional modeling.

### 4.2.2.1 Entity Relationship (ER) Modelling

ER Model is a set of concepts and graphical symbols that can be used to develop conceptual schemas. ER uses two basic concepts to produce a data model of desired business area. These concepts are Entity and Relationship between those entities. Moreover, the ER model is an abstraction tool as it can be used to identify and analyse the fuzzy relationships in the business world and complex system environment. Table 4.1 illustrates the components in ER models that consist of attributes, which can be properties that characterize either the entities or the relationships among them.

Figure 4.3 shows and example of ER diagrams. ER are a fundamental modelling technique in database design, enabling the conceptual visualization of data structures and their interrelationships within an information system. The primary

**Table 4.1** ER Concept

| Component | Definition | Example/explanation |
|---|---|---|
| Entity | An object or concept of interest to the organization that exists and can be uniquely identified. | Department, Employee, Product, Customer |
| Relationship | The structural interaction or association between entities, often represented by a line connecting two entities. Defined by **cardinality**. | An employee *belongs to* a department; a customer *purchases* a product |
| Attribute | A property or characteristic that describes or qualifies an entity. | Employee attributes: Name, ID, Position; Product attributes: Price, Category |

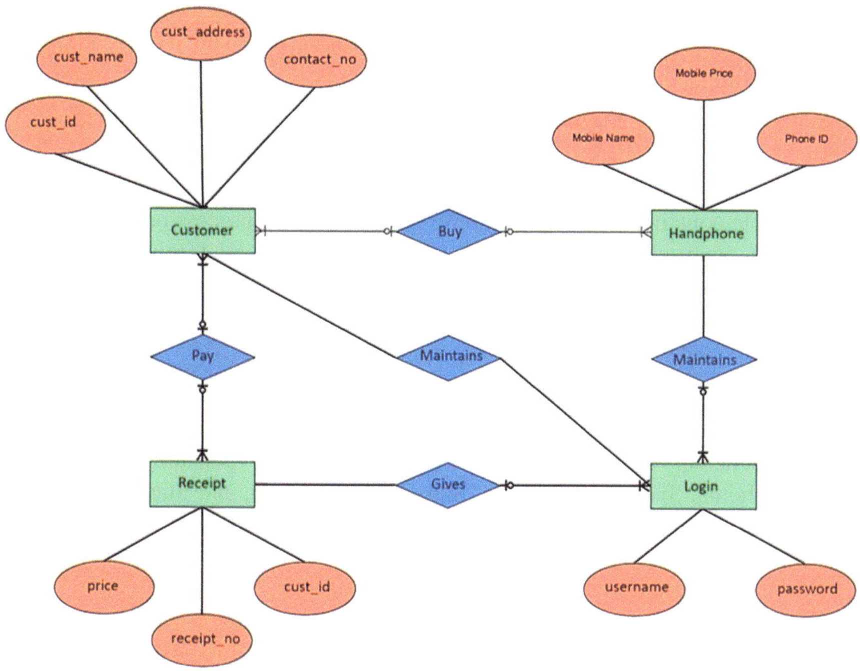


**Fig. 4.3** Example of ER model

objective of an ER diagram is to provide a high-level abstraction of the system, facilitating communication between system stakeholders, database designers, and end users.

#### 4.2.2.2 Dimensional Modelling

Dimensional modeling is a design technique used to abstract and visualize data as a collection of measures described by business-relevant features. This approach is particularly effective in capturing business requirements and translating them into database structures that align with user needs. Dimensional modeling excels in summarizing, sorting, and presenting data in analytical views, making it highly suitable for supporting data analysis.

The core concepts of dimensional modeling are dimensions, measures, and facts. This technique provides a framework that is simpler, more intuitive, and easier to comprehend than traditional entity-relationship modeling. The primary goal of dimensional modeling is to organize data in a way that facilitates efficient querying and analysis by end users.

In a dimensional model, the logical structure consists of fact tables and dimension tables. Fact tables, which often contain normalized data, represent the business processes or events being tracked, while dimension tables provide descriptive context for the facts. As an alternative to entity-relationship modeling, dimensional modeling is widely adopted in data warehousing to create data structures that are optimized for analytical performance and user accessibility.

- Dimension table records the attributes that describe the fact data. Each dimension table is assigned a unique primary key that is replicated in a fact table where it is referred to as a foreign key.
- Fact table contains measures or metrics of the business process or subject of the analysis. Fact table accommodates numerical values and foreign keys to the dimension tables. In addition to that, fact tables can record events at an atomic level of detail (as they are designed to a low level of granularity) (www.warehouseinfo.com).

The structure of a data warehouse or data mart within the framework of dimensional modeling can be represented through several distinct schema designs. These include the Flat Schema, Terraced Schema, Star Schema, Fact Constellation Schema, Galaxy Schema, Snowflake Schema, Star Cluster Schema, and Starflake Schema. Each schema offers unique characteristics and levels of complexity, suited to different analytical and business requirements.

Despite the variety of available schemas, the Star Schema and the Snowflake Schema are the two most commonly implemented models in practice. The Star Schema features a central fact table that directly links to multiple dimension tables, forming a star-like pattern. This model is favored for its simplicity, ease of understanding, and efficient query performance, making it highly accessible to business users and analysts.

In contrast, the Snowflake Schema extends the star model by further normalizing the dimension tables into additional related tables, resulting in a more complex, snowflake-like structure. This design can offer data storage efficiency and maintain data integrity by reducing redundancy, but it may introduce greater complexity in query formulation.

While various schema structures exist for modeling data warehouses and data marts, the star and snowflake schemas are the foundational approaches due to their proven effectiveness in supporting analytical operations and facilitating intuitive access to data for end users. Multidimensional Model (MDM) is a data model that structures data into facts (the subject of the analysis) and dimensions (the different perspectives to view and analyse the subject) and represent it in a star or snowflake schema. Moreover, the dimension, dimension level and dimension descriptors constitute what is referred to as dimensional concepts. These dimensional concepts form the n-dimensional data space in which the fact is placed, viewed and analysed from various perspectives. The Fig. 4.4 below illustrates a multidimensional view of sales data in data cube.

Multidimensional modeling (MDM) is widely regarded as a foundational approach for designing data warehouses, as it offers clear and intuitive data visualizations that are accessible to non-expert users. The methodologies for MDM can generally be classified into three main categories: data-driven (also called

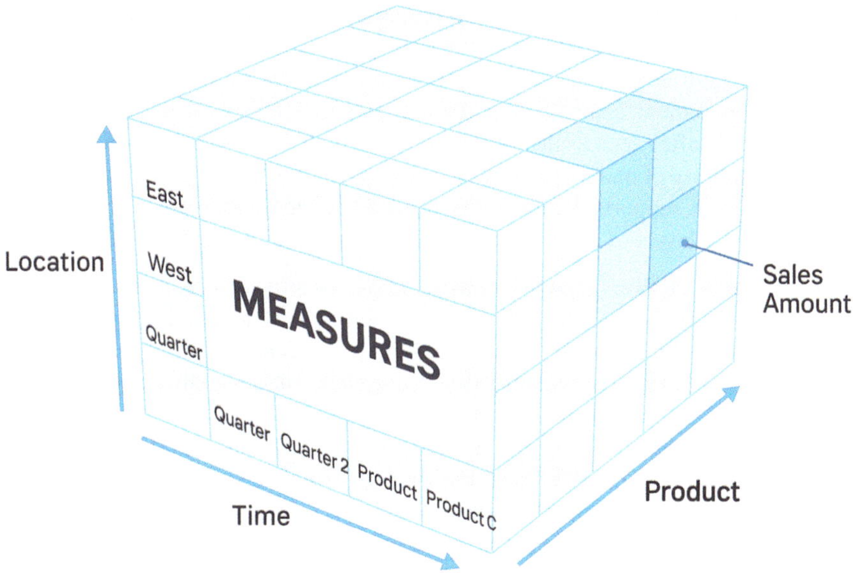


**Fig. 4.4** Data cube for sales

supply-driven), requirement-driven (also referred to as goal- or demand-driven), and hybrid frameworks.

- **Requirement-driven approach**: This method emphasizes the needs and analytical requirements of users. It starts by gathering detailed business requirements and understanding the analytical goals of the organization. The multidimensional schema is then systematically developed to reflect these requirements, ensuring that the resulting data warehouse structure aligns closely with the end users' expectations and intended use cases. This approach is similar to the process of information system design, where understanding the needs of stakeholders is a primary step before translating them into a technical solution
- **Data-driven approach**: In this approach, the focus is on the existing data within the organization. Techniques are employed to analyze and transform data stored in relational databases to uncover potential multidimensional structures. Data sources are prioritized, and the design process revolves around the available datasets. This approach is advantageous because it can reveal valuable analytical opportunities that users might not have initially identified. By leveraging well-documented data sources, data professionals can ensure the warehouse is populated with comprehensive and relevant information, sometimes uncovering hidden insights within the data that can later be leveraged for business advantage.
- **Hybrid approach:** The hybrid approach integrates both requirement-driven and data-driven methodologies. It involves designing the data warehouse with careful consideration of both the user's analytical requirements and the available data sources. This balanced framework addresses some of the limitations inherent in

relying exclusively on either approach. In practice, organizations may encounter challenges such as incomplete or poorly documented data sources, making a purely data-driven design difficult. At the same time, it is crucial to conduct thorough requirement analysis to guarantee that user needs are met. The hybrid approach is often seen as the most practical and effective solution, ensuring both the availability of quality data and the alignment of warehouse design with business goals. It supports the flexibility needed to adapt to real-world complexities and varying levels of documentation within organizational data environments.

Star Schema is a DW schema that consists of one or more central fact tables linked to numerous dimension tables. Moreover, the term star schema originated from the physical model of the schema, which looks like a star. It has a central fact table with links emanating to the surrounding dimension tables in a star shape. The Fig. 4.5 below illustrates a typical star schema.

The star schema is specifically designed to optimize query performance when working with large volumes of data. Its structure, which features a central fact table directly connected to multiple dimensions tables, minimizes the complexity of join operations. This simplicity enhances the efficiency of analytical queries, making the star schema highly suitable for use in data warehouses and data marts, particularly for supporting OLAP cubes, business intelligence tools, and advanced analytics

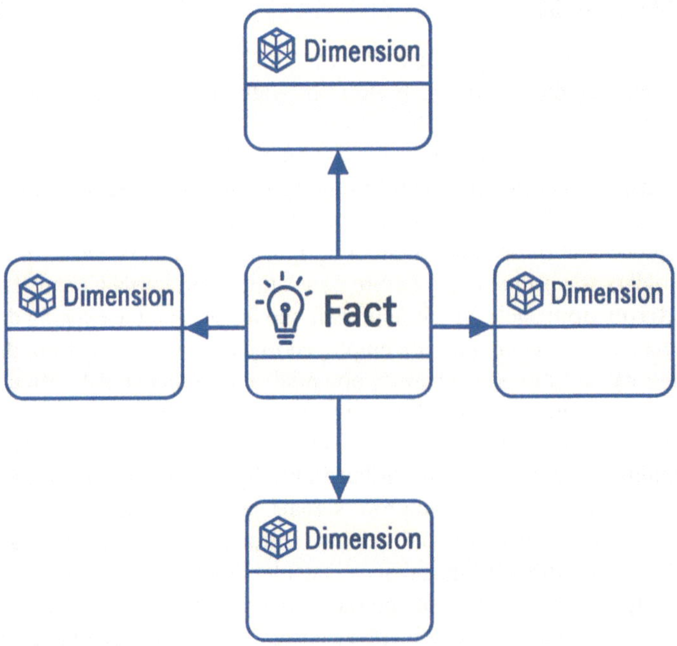


**Fig. 4.5** Star schema

applications. The straightforward arrangement of data allows for rapid aggregation, filtering, and drill-down analysis, all of which are crucial in decision support environments.

Building upon the foundation of the star schema, the snowflake schema is an extended model that introduces greater normalization to the dimension tables. In the snowflake schema, dimension tables are decomposed into multiple related tables to reduce redundancy and improve data integrity. This process involves organizing hierarchical relationships within dimensions—such as splitting a "Location" dimension into separate "Country," "Region," and "City" tables—thereby forming a structure that visually resembles a snowflake.

The snowflake schema is particularly advantageous when dimension tables contain hierarchical data or when there is a need to minimize storage by eliminating duplicate information. By normalizing dimensions, the snowflake schema enables more efficient maintenance and consistency, especially when changes need to be made across related data sets. However, this increased normalization can introduce additional complexity in query construction, as it requires more joins between tables compared to the star schema.

The star schema offers simplicity and superior performance for analytical queries, the snowflake schema extends its capabilities by supporting more complex data relationships and hierarchies through normalization. Both models play important roles in data warehousing, and the choice between them often depends on the specific analytical and operational requirements of the organization.

## 4.3 Extract Transformation Load (ETL)

The ETL process is a critical and often time-intensive component in the development of a data warehouse. This process is foundational to ensuring that the data warehouse contains high-quality, accurate, and consistent information suitable for analysis. Industry experience shows that designing and implementing ETL operations can consume a substantial proportion of project resources, often accounting for as much as 70–80% of the total time and effort required for data warehouse construction. As such, meticulous planning and specialized expertise are necessary to effectively manage this phase.

ETL is facilitated by dedicated software solutions known as ETL tools. These tools are specifically designed to automate, streamline, and manage the complex sequence of data processing steps required in data warehousing. There is a wide range of ETL tools available, both commercial and open-source, each varying in terms of features, scalability, and integration capabilities. Selecting the appropriate tool is crucial, as it directly impacts project efficiency and long-term maintainability.

**Extraction** is the initial phase, involving the collection and retrieval of data from various operational systems, which may include relational databases, legacy systems, flat files, or cloud-based sources. The main objective here is to accurately read, understand, and copy the necessary data from its original sources into a staging area temporary environment where data can be prepared for subsequent processing.

**Transformation** follows extraction and represents the most intricate stage of the ETL process. During transformation, the raw data undergoes numerous operations to ensure consistency, accuracy, and compliance with the target data warehouse's requirements. Common transformation activities include data cleansing (such as correcting spelling errors, resolving inconsistencies, and handling missing values), standardization (parsing data into uniform formats), deduplication (eliminating redundant records), integration (combining data from multiple sources), and generating surrogate keys for warehouse use. These steps are essential to harmonize data that may differ in structure, format, or semantics across diverse source systems.

**Loading** is the final stage, where the cleansed and transformed data is inserted into the data warehouse's target structures, such as fact and dimension tables. This step must be carefully managed to ensure data integrity, minimize downtime, and optimize performance, especially when dealing with large volumes of data or complex data models.

Modern ETL tools offer advanced features that greatly enhance the manageability and efficiency of the ETL process. One key feature is the metadata repository, which serves as a central catalog for synchronizing metadata between source systems, target databases, and business intelligence tools. This repository improves traceability, impact analysis, and governance. Additionally, ETL tools often include built-in schedulers that automate and orchestrate ETL workflows, making it easier to manage recurring data loads and monitor processing status.

A robust ETL solution is vital for the success of any data warehousing project. It supports the extraction, integration, and transformation of large and diverse data sets—ranging from simple transactional records to highly complex, multi-source enterprise data. By leveraging effective ETL tools and methodologies, organizations can reduce project risk, control costs, and ensure that the resulting data warehouse delivers reliable insights to meet business needs. Table 4.2 shows the list of top ETL tools in market with their main customers.

## 4.4 Building Educational Data Warehouse (EDW)

There are still limited studies for the application of BI in academic environments. Piadade and Santos introduced a concept of Student Relationship Management (SRM), an adaptation from Customer Relationship Management (CRM) concept. SRM was used to promote students' success and to closely monitor their academic activities. The CRM systems support the translation of customer information into customer knowledge. Consequently, this knowledge could be used to provide adequate strategies and actions to manage, develop and maintain stronger and profitable relationships between the enterprise and its customers. The SRM system suggested by Piadade and Santos is based on this principle and mainly supports

**Table 4.2** List top ETL tools

| ETL tool | Type | Key features | Main customers |
|---|---|---|---|
| Informatica PowerCenter | Commercial | Enterprise-scale ETL, data integration, data quality, metadata management, wide connectivity | General Electric, U.S. Bank, FedEx, Allianz, Kaiser Permanente |
| Microsoft SQL Server Integration Services (SSIS) | Commercial | Deep integration with Microsoft stack, high performance, visual workflow, data cleansing | Dell, Stack Overflow, Fidelity Investments, Accenture |
| IBM DataStage | Commercial | Parallel processing, real-time integration, strong scalability, metadata management | Citi, Vodafone, Tesco, Blue Cross Blue Shield |
| Talend Data Integration | Open Source/ Commercial | Open-source core, advanced data integration, cloud support, Big Data, rich connectors | AstraZeneca, ABInBev, Lenovo, Air France |
| Oracle Data Integrator (ODI) | Commercial | High performance, support for Oracle and non-Oracle sources, ELT architecture | Vodafone, Schneider Electric, Halliburton, Orange S.A. |
| Apache Nifi | Open Source | Real-time data ingestion, flow-based programming, IoT/ streaming support | Cloudera, HCA Healthcare, National Security Agency (NSA) |
| Fivetran | Commercial (Cloud) | Automated schema management, zero-maintenance, cloud-native, connectors for SaaS and databases | Square, DocuSign, Strava, Autodesk |
| Matillion | Commercial (Cloud) | Native integration with AWS, Google Cloud, Snowflake, ELT processing for cloud DWH | Siemens, Cisco, TUI Group, Slack |
| AWS Glue | Cloud Native | Serverless, managed ETL, deep AWS ecosystem integration, auto-scaling, pay-per-use | News Corp, Toyota, Expedia Group, twenty-first Century Fox |
| SAP Data Services | Commercial | Comprehensive ETL, enterprise data quality, integration with SAP landscape | Bosch, Mercedes-Benz, Siem |

activities related with the students and those particularly associated with the teaching and learning process. BI technology has been proposed as the main pillar technology to support SRM.

In our past research, we have proposed an Educational Intelligence (EI) Concept to effectively manage data in an academic environment. The EI model combines technologies, tools, and technique, people (students, academia, and other stakeholders) to achieve constructive knowledge that helps improve teaching and learning process. Figure 4.6 illustrates the general idea of EI fundamental framework where Educational Data Warehouse (EDW) is the main component to support EI concept.

In 2012, Chen further advanced the concept of Educational Intelligence (EI) in his master's research thesis, "Applying Business Intelligence in Higher Education

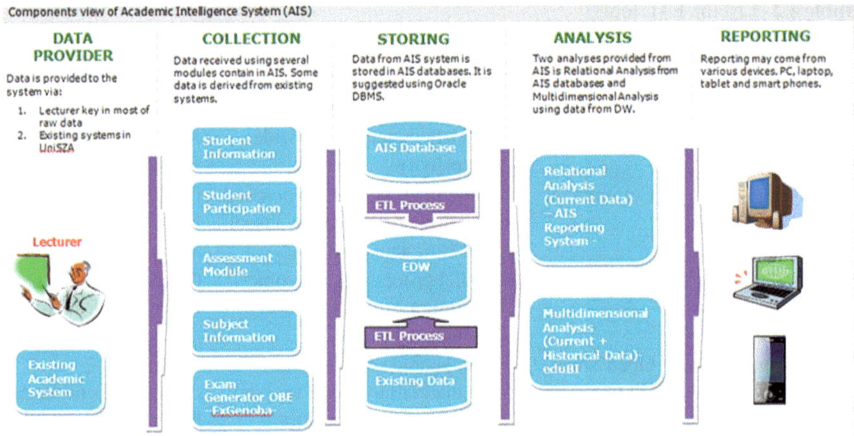


**Fig. 4.6** Educational Intelligence (EI) framework

Sector: Conceptual Models and Users Acceptance." In this work, Chen introduced several enhancements to the EI framework to increase its applicability and relevance for Higher Education Institutions (HEIs). He also explored various factors that influence users' acceptance and adoption of EI systems within academic environments.

The EDW serves as the foundational framework for developing data warehouses specifically for the educational domain, with a focus on analyzing student performance. The EDW acts as the backend infrastructure for an EI framework, supporting the integration and storage of comprehensive academic data. On the other hand, the front-end component is known as Educational Business Intelligence (EduBI), which leverages business intelligence technologies to unify disparate academic data sources into a single, consolidated repository (the EDW).

While the majority of business intelligence literature has its roots in the corporate sector, IT industry, and software vendors, academic research—particularly in the context of information retrieval and educational analytics—remains in a nascent stage. EDW provides timely access to critical academic metrics, enabling institutions to monitor and assess student achievement across various programs and curricula. Data such as students' examination results, sourced from multiple platforms, can be extracted, transformed, and loaded into a multidimensional model to support advanced OLAP (Online Analytical Processing) queries.

Once this data is structured within the EDW, educational stakeholders can apply BI technologies—such as analytical reporting, dashboards, and OLAP tools—to conduct in-depth analyses of students' academic performance. These application components collectively form the EduBI layer, dedicated to the interpretation and visualization of student data for decision-making and continuous improvement.

From a data modeling perspective, the design of the EDW typically involves using students' academic results as the central fact table, surrounded by several related dimension tables. Figure 4.7 demonstrates this multidimensional model.

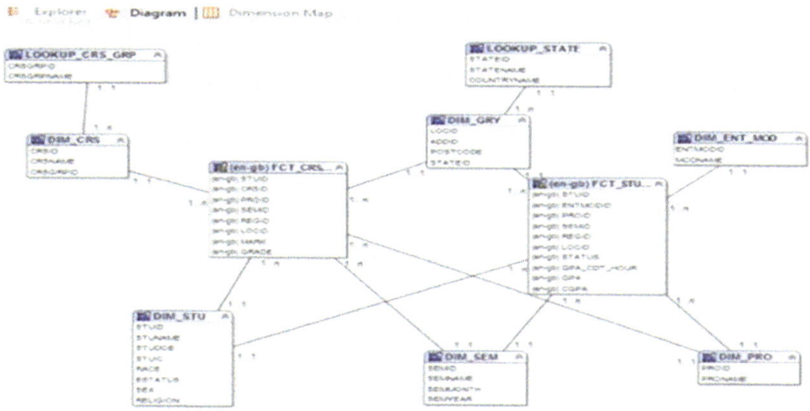


**Fig. 4.7** EDW multidimensional design (redraw table)

Unlike traditional data warehouses that primarily focus on data aggregation and summarization, the core challenge in educational data modeling lies in the need to retain detailed, granular student information. To effectively predict and analyze academic outcomes, it is essential to capture and store comprehensive data for each student—such as assignment marks, attendance records, final examination scores, and other pertinent attributes. This level of detail supports a deeper, more accurate analysis of student performance and educational outcomes.

The main facts tables in the model are Fact Course Result (FCT_CRS_RES) and Fact Student Result (FCT_STU_RES). The FCT_CRS_RES table contains the root items of students' detailed examination results for particular subjects. The measured values in the table are students' final marks for respective subjects. In addition, it also stores the corresponding grade. The FCT_STU_RES table contains only GPA and CGPA for the current semester. Both GPA and CGPA were the measured values of the table. Both facts tables link to 6 dimensions tables (student dimension, location dimension, time/semester dimension, program dimension, course dimension).

The data available in EDW will be used for analytical purposes. OLAP application has been used to provide the descriptive analysis. Through this application, the details of student performances over a subject and student achievement records can be obtained. For example, a query to obtain student performance on a specific subject group based on certain amount of time can be triggered by combining Subject Dimension ($D_{SUB}$), Time Dimension ($D_{TIME}$) and Student Dimension ($D_{STU}$) with Fact ($F_{RES}$).

Some major analyses can be derived from the EDW model:

1. Student Achievement Analysis based on subject group

   The objective of this analysis is to obtain the best subject group of students. Based on Information Technology (IT) subject groups (networking, multimedia, software engineering, programming and databases), the graph from the analysis of results can be produced to perform the comparison and to view students' progressive achievements. Knowing the best subject group is important in order to suggest the best computer field for the students to further their studies. In addition, performing mining techniques to find the reason/s of each student's improvement or vice versa can be done. The fact result has many to one relation with dimension assessment. Each student's assessment (number of quiz taken, attendance, number of assignments done, and frequency of meeting lecturer) will be recorded to know whether the assessment can help the students improve their grades.

2. Clustering Analysis

   Clustering is a process of grouping physical or abstract objects into classes of similar oobjects. Clustering and classification are both classification method; clustering is an unsupervised classification and classification is a supervised classification [15]. The goal of the clustering technique is descriptive rather than predictive [8]. It can be done by categorizing students into homogenous groups such as groups of programs (multimedia & IT), gender or pointer. Identifying students based on the similar group can help researchers perform more specific analysis against the group. Thus, a decision can be made for choosing the best learning method to be applied to a particular group of students. Talavera & Gaudiso [7] have conducted the cluster profiling in mining students' data in E-Learning environment.

3. Predictive Analysis

   Predictive analysis is a process of predicting the patterns or future results based on current data available. It is important in the Decision Support System (DSS) to make better decisions based on existing data.

## 4.5 Chapter Conclusion

In this chapter, we explored the essential components of building a data warehouse (DW) for higher education, emphasizing its role in supporting data-driven decision-making across institutional functions. The discussion began with an introduction to data warehousing, highlighting its importance in consolidating disparate data sources to enhance reporting, analytics, and strategic planning in higher education institutions (HEIs).

We then examined the fundamentals of data warehouses, distinguishing them from traditional databases and operational systems. The chapter further delved into different DW approaches, such as top-down, bottom-up, and hybrid models, each offering unique advantages based on institutional needs and available resources.

A key focus was placed on DW modeling techniques, including star schema, snowflake schema, and fact constellation, which provide structured methods for organizing and retrieving educational data efficiently. Understanding these models is crucial in optimizing data retrieval for reporting, analytics, and institutional research.

The Extract, Transform, Load (ETL) process was also analyzed in detail, covering data extraction from multiple sources, transformation into a consistent format, and loading into the data warehouse. This step is critical in ensuring data quality, integrity, and accuracy for higher education analytics.

Finally, we synthesized these concepts in the Building an Educational Data Warehouse (EDW) section, outlining the best practices, challenges, and implementation strategies tailored to the needs of HEIs. The discussion underscored the significance of scalability, security, and governance in designing an EDW that serves multiple stakeholders, including administrators, faculty, and policymakers.

# Chapter 5
# Data Visualization and Reporting

## 5.1 Introduction

In today's world, where data plays a key role in decision-making, organizations depend more than ever on large amounts of information to shape their strategies, streamline operations, and stay competitive. But raw data can be overwhelming, making it hard to make sense of or use effectively. This is where data visualization becomes essential. By turning complex data into visual formats—like charts, graphs, and dashboards—visualization makes it easier to spot trends, recognize patterns, and clearly communicate insights to stakeholders. In Chap. 5, we'll look at how important data visualization is for decision-making, explore key design principles for creating effective visuals, and examine how to build interactive dashboards and reports tailored to different users.

## 5.2 The Importance of Data Visualization

Data visualization plays a crucial role in helping organizations make informed, data-driven decisions by turning raw, often complex data into easily digestible visual formats. The primary value of visualization is that it enables users to quickly understand key insights and trends, facilitating more effective and timely decision-making processes. Rather than sifting through dense spreadsheets or lengthy reports, decision-makers can grasp critical information at a glance through well-designed visuals.

1. **Simplifying Complex Data:** One of the greatest challenges in data-driven environments is managing and interpreting large datasets. Data visualization simplifies this process by transforming complex numerical data into visual elements,



A. A. Aziz et al., *Business Intelligence for Higher Education*,
https://doi.org/10.1007/978-3-032-05361-9_5

such as bar charts, line graphs, and heatmaps, that are easier to comprehend. This reduction in cognitive load allows users to identify trends, outliers, and correlations faster, enhancing their ability to make strategic decisions.

2. **Improved Communication:** Visualizations also serve as a universal language, facilitating clearer communication between data analysts and non-technical stakeholders. By translating raw data into visuals, reports and presentations become more engaging and understandable, allowing a broader audience to grasp insights. This is especially useful in cross-functional teams where different departments rely on varying levels of technical expertise. Data visualizations enable alignment on key metrics and goals across the organization.
3. **Real-Time Insights:** In today's fast-paced business environment, the ability to make timely decisions is paramount. Data visualization tools, particularly those integrated with live data streams, allow organizations to monitor key performance indicators (KPIs) and business metrics in real-time. This enables decision-makers to respond quickly to emerging trends or operational issues, minimizing the time lag between data analysis and action.
4. **Enhanced Strategic Planning:** By providing a clear picture of historical performance and current trends, data visualization supports long-term strategic planning. Decision-makers can use visual tools to forecast future outcomes, identify potential risks, and evaluate different scenarios. Visual representations of data make it easier to communicate these strategies to stakeholders, ensuring that everyone involved has a clear understanding of the company's direction.
5. **Driving Engagement and Action:** Visualizing data not only helps to communicate information but also motivates action. Data stories told through visualizations are more engaging and impactful than mere numbers or textual reports. When decision-makers can clearly see the impact of their actions—whether it's through improving customer satisfaction scores or increasing revenue—they are more likely to take action based on the insights provided.

## 5.3 Dashboard Design Principles

The importance of data visualization in decision-making cannot be overstated. It bridges the gap between data complexity and clarity, allowing organizations to unlock the full potential of their data for more informed and timely decisions. Whether it's simplifying intricate datasets, fostering better communication across teams, or enabling real-time insights, data visualization is essential for driving effective decision-making and fostering a data-centric culture within organizations.

### 5.3.1 *Effective Information Presentation*

A successful BI dashboard begins with a thorough understanding of the end user, considering their role, analytical proficiency, and the specific ways in which data can enhance their decision-making processes and operational actions. It is critical to identify not only the type of insights the users require but also how they interpret and interact with data, ensuring that the information presented is both relevant and actionable.

Once these user-specific requirements are defined, the dashboard must be tailored accordingly—whether it is a strategic dashboard offering high-level, long-term insights or an operational dashboard focused on real-time, actionable metrics. The design of the dashboard should intuitively guide the user through the data exploration process, allowing them to seamlessly navigate from raw data to critical insights. This involves carefully structuring visual elements, such as charts, graphs, and key performance indicators (KPIs), in a manner that prioritizes clarity, reduces cognitive load, and supports efficient decision-making.

Incorporating best practices for data visualization is essential. For example, using appropriate color schemes, consistent labeling, and data hierarchy aids in drawing attention to the most important information without overwhelming the user. Furthermore, the layout must be adaptable, ensuring the dashboard is accessible across various devices and platforms while maintaining the integrity of the data presentation. By focusing on these principles, the dashboard becomes a tool that not only displays data but also transforms it into actionable intelligence. Figure 5.1 shows examples integrating and visualizing data using dashboard and combining BI features elements.

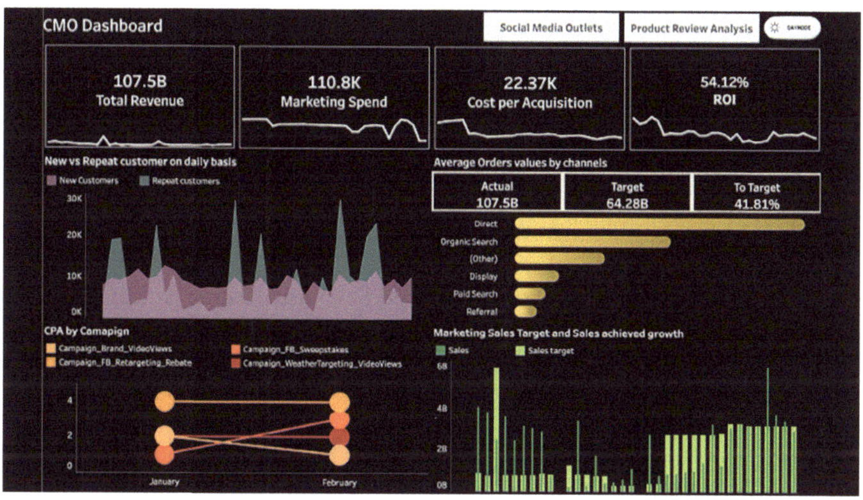


**Fig. 5.1** Example of dashboard design

### 5.3.2 *Visual Consistency*

Achieving clarity in dashboard design is fundamentally dependent on the consistent use of visual elements such as typography, color schemes, and graphical components. Consistency across these design aspects ensures that the dashboard remains intuitive and easy to navigate, reducing the cognitive effort required for users to interpret the data. Typography, for instance, should be uniform in size and style, with headings, subheadings, and body text clearly differentiated to establish a visual hierarchy that guides the user's attention.

The use of color should be similarly deliberate and consistent. Colors can be powerful tools for categorizing data, highlighting key metrics, and indicating trends, but they must be applied thoughtfully to avoid confusion or distraction. A cohesive color palette not only enhances the visual appeal of the dashboard but also aids in directing the user's focus to the most important insights. Color associations should remain uniform throughout the interface—e.g., using specific colors to denote positive and negative trends or to distinguish between different data categories.

Graphic elements such as icons, borders, and spacing must also be standardized to ensure a seamless user experience. Visual consistency helps create a design language that users can subconsciously rely on as they navigate the dashboard, allowing them to focus more on deriving insights from the data rather than on deciphering the interface itself.

Moreover, maintaining a consistent visual hierarchy in the presentation of elements helps prioritize information effectively. Critical data points should stand out, while supplementary or less urgent data can be de-emphasized. This structured approach to design leads to a cohesive and professional dashboard experience, where each element contributes purposefully to the user's data exploration and decision-making process. By adhering to these principles, the design supports the dashboard's core function of transforming complex data into accessible, actionable insights.

### 5.3.3 *Efficient Interactions*

An efficient dashboard design is not about displaying as much information as possible, but about presenting data that is essential, relevant, and easily digestible. Overloading the dashboard with every report or visualization at your disposal detracts from its usability. Just because a particular dataset or visualization is accessible does not mean it needs to be included. Every element in the dashboard should serve a clear purpose, contributing to the specific needs of the end-user and their decision-making process.

Any visualizations that do not directly support these goals should be eliminated to maintain a clean and focused interface. Removing unnecessary components reduces clutter and cognitive overload, allowing users to concentrate on the most critical insights. A well-constructed dashboard provides the user with a clear path to actionable data without overwhelming them with extraneous information.

Equally important is the design and placement of filters, actions, and interactive elements, which should seamlessly align with the user's workflow. These features should be intuitive and accessible, enabling users to refine data views, explore deeper insights, or adjust parameters with minimal effort. Filters should be designed to logically follow the user's thought process, making it easy to drill down into specific data subsets or switch between different perspectives.

Moreover, interactive elements must be designed for efficiency. Actions such as data filtering, sorting, or exporting should happen quickly and fluidly, without disrupting the user's experience. Dashboards should respond dynamically to user inputs, ensuring that every interaction adds value and supports the flow of data exploration. By focusing on simplicity, clarity, and alignment with user goals, efficient dashboard interactions enhance both the functionality and the overall user experience, transforming complex datasets into manageable and actionable insights.

### 5.3.4 *Effective Use of Languages*

Language plays a critical role in dashboard design, functioning as an essential tool for user experience alongside visual elements like color, font, and style. Clear, concise, and well-considered language ensures that users can navigate complex visualizations and layouts with ease. Just as visual consistency helps users interpret data efficiently, effective use of language—through labels, notes, and explanations—provides essential context that guides users through their data exploration journey.

Labeling should be precise and unambiguous, helping users instantly understand the purpose of each chart, graph, or data point. Consistent and intuitive labels eliminate guesswork, allowing the user to focus on analyzing data rather than interpreting the interface. Furthermore, well-placed notes and tooltips can provide additional context without overwhelming the primary visualization, offering users deeper insights when needed.

Language can also help bridge the gap between different levels of user expertise. Whether the end-users are data-savvy analysts or business professionals with limited technical knowledge, the use of clear, non-technical language ensures that the dashboard remains accessible to all. For more complex or technical terms, explanatory notes can be integrated to guide users through advanced data concepts without disrupting the dashboard's flow.

Moreover, the tone and clarity of language should align with the overall design goals of the dashboard. If the dashboard is used for high-level strategic decisions, the language should reflect that by being succinct yet informative. In contrast, operational dashboards that support real-time decision-making may require more detailed explanations to ensure that users can act quickly and with confidence.

Ultimately, the use of language in dashboard design should enhance the user's ability to interpret and interact with the data. When employed thoughtfully, language functions as a subtle guide, making complex data comprehensible and actionable, while ensuring that users remain engaged and focused on extracting meaningful insights.

### 5.3.5 *Minimize the Cognitive Load*

A well-designed dashboard succeeds when it minimizes the cognitive load required for users to interpret and interact with the data. Cognitive load refers to the mental effort needed to process information, and dashboards that are overly complex or cluttered can overwhelm users, reducing their ability to draw meaningful insights efficiently. Without realizing it, users will naturally gravitate away from interfaces that are mentally taxing, opting for those that feel more intuitive and less demanding.

While visual aesthetics are often emphasized in design, the primary goal should be to create an interface that is not only visually appealing but also "mentally" comfortable. A good design doesn't just look good—it feels good to use. This means structuring the dashboard in a way that reduces friction, allowing users to focus on the data rather than how to navigate the interface. Simplified layouts, consistent patterns, and clear data hierarchies all contribute to reducing the mental effort required to interpret the information.

Minimizing cognitive load involves eliminating unnecessary complexity. Overloading the dashboard with excessive information, intricate visualizations, or ambiguous labels can lead to confusion and frustration. Instead, dashboards should follow a minimalist approach, where each element serves a purpose and supports the user's data journey. Grouping related information together, providing clear labels, and using intuitive visual metaphors help users process data quickly and make informed decisions without unnecessary strain.

Ultimately, a design that minimizes cognitive load creates an environment where users can engage with the dashboard effortlessly. This balance between visual clarity and mental ease leads to a more satisfying user experience, where the interface serves as a transparent medium for interacting with complex data. When the dashboard is both aesthetically pleasing and mentally intuitive, users can concentrate on what matters most—making data-driven decisions with confidence and efficiency.

## 5.4 Key Performance Indicators (KPI)

In the current era of digital transformation, organizations across all sectors increasingly rely on data-driven strategies to maintain competitiveness and achieve operational excellence. At the heart of effective performance management are Key Performance Indicators (KPIs), which serve as quantifiable metrics reflecting critical success factors within an organization. KPIs play a pivotal role in translating organizational strategy into actionable objectives, enabling continuous monitoring, evaluation, and optimization of performance at all levels. Indicators are a measurable value that demonstrates how effectively an organization, department, or individual is achieving key business objectives. KPIs are not merely data points; they are strategically selected metrics that align with the mission and vision of the organization, serving as a compass for decision-makers.

Characteristics of Effective KPIs rely on SMART concepts, which are:

- **Strategic Alignment:** Directly linked to organizational goals.
- **Measurable:** Quantifiable and trackable over time.
- **Actionable:** Provide insight that informs decision-making and actions.
- **Relevant:** Focused on critical success factors.
- **Timely:** Available at intervals that allow for timely intervention.

In other perceptive, dashboards for KPI need to be interactive, real-time visual displays that consolidate and present critical KPIs and metrics in a single view. They enable organizations to monitor performance continuously and respond promptly to emerging trends or issues.

- Key Functions of Dashboards:
- Real-Time Monitoring: Dashboards aggregate data from multiple sources, providing up-to-date information on key indicators.
- Visual Clarity: Use of charts, graphs, trend lines, and heat maps to simplify complex data.
- Customizability: Users can tailor dashboard views to focus on metrics most relevant to their roles.
- Drill-Down Capability: Advanced dashboards allow users to explore data at various levels of detail for root-cause analysis.

Scorecards are management tools that track performance against strategic objectives over time. While dashboards are often used for operational monitoring, scorecards focus on alignment with broader organizational strategy.

Key Elements of Scorecards:

- Comparative Tracking: Visual comparisons against targets, benchmarks, or historical performance.
- Strategic Hierarchies: Scorecards can cascade KPIs from organizational goals down to individual or departmental metrics.
- Accountability: Assigns ownership to KPIs, reinforcing responsibility for outcomes.
- Periodic Review: Facilitates regular performance reviews and strategic planning.

As example, university scorecard may track graduation rates, student satisfaction, and research output against strategic goals, allowing leaders to compare actual performance to institutional benchmarks as shown in Fig. 5.2.

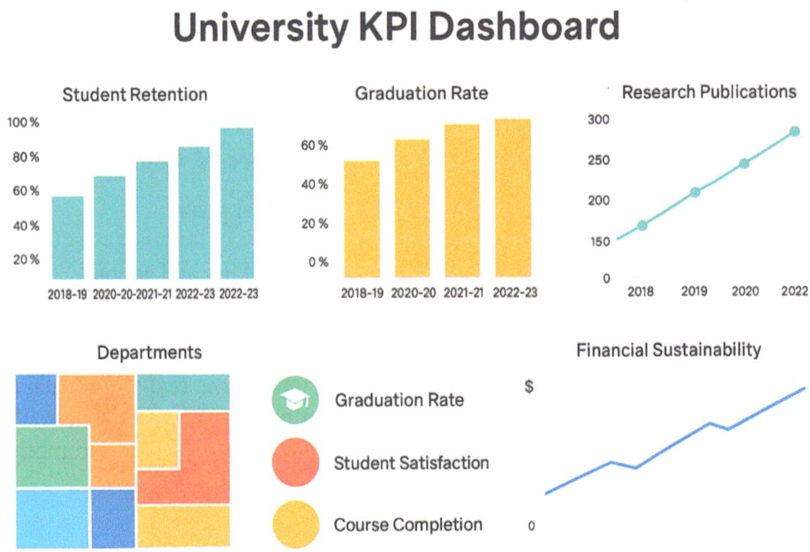


**Fig. 5.2** Example of KPI in education context

### 5.4.1 *Effective KPI*

The adoption of effective Key Performance Indicator (KPI) frameworks has become central to organizational excellence across sectors, including higher education. KPIs serve as quantifiable measures that reflect the critical success factors of an institution, transforming abstract strategic goals into actionable metrics. By systematically capturing and analyzing performance data, KPI frameworks provide academic leaders with a robust mechanism for evaluating institutional effectiveness, fostering a culture of evidence-based management, and supporting both short-term and long-term strategic planning (Kaplan & Norton, 1996; Marr, 2015).

Central to the impact of effective KPI frameworks is their integration with real-time dashboards and balanced scorecards. Dashboards offer dynamic visualizations of key metrics, granting stakeholders immediate access to relevant and up-to-date performance insights. Scorecards, on the other hand, facilitate the alignment of departmental and individual objectives with broader organizational strategy. The synergy between these tools ensures that decision-making processes are transparent, data-driven, and closely aligned with institutional priorities. Furthermore, by enabling timely identification of trends, risks, and opportunities, these systems enhance institutional agility and responsiveness in an increasingly complex environment (Eckerson, 2010; Parmenter, 2015).

Beyond operational benefits, effective KPI frameworks are instrumental in cultivating a culture of accountability and continuous improvement. Transparent reporting of key metrics not only builds trust among stakeholders but also encourages ongoing performance optimization through iterative feedback loops. This continuous review and refinement process empowers higher education institutions to address performance gaps proactively, respond to stakeholder needs, and pursue excellence in teaching, research, and community engagement (De Waal, 2013). Through such systematic approaches, KPIs evolve from mere measurement tools to strategic levers that drive sustainable organizational success.

To summarize effective KPI frameworks, when supported by dashboards and scorecards divided into:

- **Enhanced Decision-Making:** Timely and relevant KPI insights guide leaders in making informed decisions.
- **Increased Transparency:** Open visibility into key metrics fosters a culture of accountability and trust.
- **Agility and Responsiveness:** Real-time data empowers organizations to adapt quickly to market changes or operational challenges.
- **Continuous Improvement:** KPIs highlight areas for improvement, enabling targeted interventions and ongoing optimization.
- **Alignment of Objectives:** Scorecards ensure that departmental and individual efforts align with organizational strategy.

### *5.4.2 KPI Framework in Higher Education*

In the context of higher education, a robust KPI framework is instrumental for institutional leaders seeking to ensure accountability, enhance quality, and drive continuous improvement. As universities and colleges face increasing demands for transparency, resource optimization, and student-centric outcomes, KPIs serve as vital tools to measure, monitor, and communicate progress towards strategic objectives.

A comprehensive KPI framework in higher education typically encompasses the following dimensions:

- Student Success and Progression
  - Retention Rate: Percentage of students who continue from one academic year to the next.
  - Graduation Rate: Proportion of students completing programs within the expected timeframe.
  - Course Completion Rate: Measures successful completion of individual courses.
  - Average GPA: Indicates overall academic performance.
- Teaching and Learning Quality

  - Student Satisfaction: Results from surveys on teaching quality, learning environment, and support services.
  - Faculty-to-Student Ratio: Proxy for instructional quality and access to faculty.
  - Assessment Scores: Benchmarking against accreditation or licensure exams.

- Research and Innovation
  - Research Output: Number of published papers, citations, and patents.
  - External Grant Funding: Value and number of grants secured.
  - Industry Collaborations: Partnerships, internships, and commercialization projects.

- Operational and Financial Performance
  - Budget Utilization: Effective management of allocated funds.
  - Infrastructure Utilization: Usage rates of campus facilities and digital platforms.
  - Cost per Graduate: Financial efficiency in producing qualified graduates.

- Graduate Employability
  - Employment Rate: Proportion of graduates employed within six months of graduation.
  - Further Study Rate: Number of graduates progressing to postgraduate education.
  - Employer Satisfaction: Feedback from employers on graduate preparedness.

The process of implementing a KPI framework in higher education involves several key steps:

(a) Strategic Alignment:
KPIs must directly reflect the institution's mission, vision, and strategic plan. For example, a university aiming to be a leader in research will emphasize research output and funding KPIs.

(b) Data Integration:
Data is sourced from multiple systems—student information systems (SIS), learning management systems (LMS), finance, HR, and alumni databases—and integrated into a unified data warehouse or analytics platform.

(c) Visualization and Dashboards:
KPIs are displayed through interactive dashboards, enabling stakeholders at all levels—executives, deans, faculty, and administrative staff—to monitor progress. Dashboards may feature traffic light indicators, trend lines, comparative scorecards, and real-time alerts for underperformance or achievement of targets.

(d) Governance and Accountability:
Clear ownership of each KPI is established, with regular review meetings to assess progress and implement corrective actions.

(e) Continuous Improvement:

KPI results inform data-driven decision-making, supporting strategic planning, resource allocation, and policy revisions.

### 5.4.3 Case Study in IHLS

The subsequent subsections are dedicated to an in-depth case study examining the implementation of Key Performance Indicator (KPI) practices within Institutions of Higher Learning (IHLs). Through this focused analysis, the discussion will elucidate how various IHLs have operationalized KPI frameworks to monitor, assess, and enhance institutional performance across critical domains such as academic achievement, research output, student engagement, and administrative efficiency. Drawing on empirical data and best practices, each sub-point will explore specific strategies, challenges encountered, and outcomes achieved in the application of KPI methodologies. This case-based approach not only highlights the practical realities of KPI adoption in the higher education sector but also offers insights into the mechanisms by which these institutions align performance measurement with strategic objectives, foster a culture of accountability, and drive continuous improvement

#### 5.4.3.1 Havard University

Harvard University, as a globally recognized leader in higher education, has institutionalized the use of KPIs to align its academic, research, and operational objectives with its long-term strategic vision. Harvard's KPI framework spans across faculties, administrative departments, and institutional priorities.

KPI Framework Implementation

*Strategic Planning*

Harvard's Office of Institutional Research (OIR) collaborates with leadership teams to develop strategic KPIs supporting Harvard's mission. These KPIs cover academic excellence, research output, diversity, financial sustainability, and student success.

*Examples of KPIs Used*

- Graduation and Retention Rates: Continuously tracked across all schools.
- Research Productivity: Number and quality of publications, citation indices, grant acquisition.
- Faculty Diversity: Percentage of faculty from underrepresented groups.
- Student Satisfaction and Engagement: Surveys measuring student experiences.
- Operational Efficiency: Metrics on resource allocation and cost-effectiveness.

*Data Visualization*

Interactive dashboards (often built with tools such as Tableau and Power BI) provide real-time and longitudinal views, enabling academic leaders and faculty to drill down into departmental, program, and demographic trends.

*Continuous Improvement*

KPI results are reviewed regularly at multiple levels (university, school, department), driving targeted interventions such as curriculum enhancements, support services, and policy changes.

*Public Reporting*

Harvard's "Fact Book" and annual reports publish selected KPIs for transparency and accountability to stakeholders, donors, and accreditation bodies.

*Impact*

Harvard's KPI framework has supported strategic decisions, such as targeted recruitment, faculty hiring, and research investments. For example, continuous monitoring of diversity KPIs has informed more inclusive hiring practices and student outreach programs. Transparent reporting of graduation rates and financial indicators ensures sustained donor confidence and institutional reputation.

#### 5.4.3.2 Universiti Malaya

Universiti Malaya (UM), Malaysia's premier public research university, systematically employs KPI frameworks to achieve its goal of being a world-class institution. As a research-intensive university, UM aligns its KPIs with the Malaysian Ministry of Higher Education's performance indicators and global ranking criteria.

Strategic Alignment

UM's KPIs are structured around its strategic plan and government's National Higher Education Strategic Plan. Key domains include teaching and learning, research, internationalization, graduate employability, and financial management.

Examples of KPIs Used

- Research Output: Number of SCOPUS/WoS-indexed publications, patents filed, citations.

- Student Employability: Percentage of graduates employed within six months post-graduation.
- Global Rankings: Scores and movements in QS, THE, and other international rankings.
- Academic Quality: Student-to-staff ratio, program accreditation rates.
- International Collaboration: Number of international joint publications, MoUs, inbound/outbound mobility.

For data integration and visualization: UM has invested in an integrated data warehouse and analytics platform. Real-time dashboards and scorecards are used by top management, deans, and department heads to monitor progress and benchmark against targets.

Actionable Insights and Reviews

KPI data drives annual faculty reviews, resource allocation, and targeted interventions (e.g., research funding, curriculum reform, academic staff development).

External Reporting

KPI results are submitted to the Ministry of Higher Education and published in UM's Annual Report and Quality Assurance self-assessment documents.

UM's systematic KPI monitoring has resulted in significant improvements in research output, graduate employability, and international recognition. The university's strong focus on research KPIs has helped it remain Malaysia's top-ranked institution, achieving top 100 status in several QS subject areas. Real-time monitoring allows UM to respond rapidly to underperforming units and recognize high achievers.

#### 5.4.3.3 University of Melbourne

The University of Melbourne is internationally recognized for academic excellence and research impact. To sustain its global competitiveness and support strategic growth, the university relies on a comprehensive KPI framework integrated across academic and administrative units.

KPI Framework Implementation

*Strategic Integration*

The university's KPIs are tightly coupled with the institutional strategic plan, covering areas such as student experience, research quality, graduate outcomes, sustainability, and community engagement.

*Examples of KPIs Used*

- Student Satisfaction Scores: Results from annual university-wide surveys.
- Graduate Employment Rates: Percentage of graduates in full-time employment within six months.
- Research Impact: Citations per publication, grant funding, research commercialization.
- Sustainability Metrics: Campus energy usage, waste reduction, carbon footprint.
- Diversity and Inclusion: Representation of underrepresented groups among students and staff.

*Data Visualization*

The Office of Planning and Performance produces interactive dashboards (using tools like Tableau and Power BI), enabling executives and academic leaders to monitor KPIs in real-time, compare with historical data, and benchmark against peer institutions.

*Accountability and Review*

Each academic division has ownership of relevant KPIs and is required to submit periodic progress reports. Regular performance review meetings facilitate discussion of gaps, best practices, and corrective measures.

*Continuous Improvement*

Insights gained from KPI dashboards drive resource allocation, curriculum reform, and targeted student support programs.

Through its KPI framework, the University of Melbourne has achieved sustained improvement in student engagement, increased research funding, and enhanced global rankings. Transparent reporting has fostered a culture of accountability and collective ownership of outcomes.

## 5.5 Chapter Conclusion

In this chapter, we delved deeply into the pivotal function of data visualization and reporting within the context of Business Intelligence (BI) in higher education. As universities and colleges continue to amass vast and diverse datasets—from student enrolment figures to faculty research outputs—translating this raw information into meaningful, accessible insights has become increasingly crucial. Effective data representation bridges the gap between data complexity and institutional action, empowering leaders, administrators, and academic staff to make well-informed, evidence-based decisions at all levels.

We began with an introduction to data visualization, underscoring its importance in simplifying intricate datasets and enhancing users' ability to detect patterns, trends, and outliers. Visualizations such as interactive dashboards, heatmaps, and trend lines not only make large datasets more comprehensible but also support data-driven storytelling—a powerful approach for engaging stakeholders and communicating key findings. Through the use of modern BI tools, universities can now present information in dynamic formats that encourage exploration and foster collaborative decision-making.

The chapter also distinguished between the main types of BI-driven reporting in higher education: operational, analytical, and strategic. Operational reports focus on day-to-day activities and immediate needs, such as class attendance or real-time campus resource utilization. Analytical reports delve deeper, providing multi-dimensional analysis to uncover underlying factors that affect institutional performance—such as analyzing student performance by demographic group or program. Strategic reports, meanwhile, aggregate high-level metrics that guide long-term planning and policy formulation, aligning institutional objectives with measurable outcomes.

Moreover, we explored the rise of automated reporting systems powered by BI platforms. These systems enable the seamless delivery of real-time analytics, drastically reducing manual reporting efforts and minimizing delays in critical decision-making. With the ability to monitor key performance indicators (KPIs)—including student retention rates, graduation rates, financial health, and faculty productivity—in near real-time, higher education institutions can swiftly identify issues, benchmark progress, and adapt strategies as needed.

In summary, data visualization and BI-driven reporting have become indispensable tools for higher education institutions seeking to foster a culture of evidence-based management. By transforming complex data into actionablc insights and enabling timely, transparent reporting, these tools support not only operational excellence, but also long-term strategic success in an increasingly data-driven academic landscape.

# Chapter 6
# Enhancing Student Success with BI

## 6.1 Introduction

In today's dynamic higher education environment, the ability to make data-informed decisions has become essential for institutions striving to improve student outcomes. Business Intelligence (BI) offers a comprehensive solution for leveraging data to drive student success, empowering educators and administrators to enhance retention rates, graduation rates, and overall academic performance. Through the application of BI tools and analytics, institutions can gain a deeper understanding of student behaviours, challenges, and success factors, ultimately creating more effective strategies for fostering academic achievement.

One of the most significant benefits of BI in education is its potential to improve student retention and graduation rates. High attrition rates are a challenge for many institutions, often leading to lost revenue and diminished student success. By utilizing BI, schools can analyse a wide array of data sources, such as enrolment trends, attendance records, and student engagement metrics, to identify key factors that contribute to student dropout. BI tools can detect patterns and trends that might not be obvious through traditional reporting methods, allowing institutions to pinpoint where students are most likely to disengage and intervene before it's too late. By taking a proactive, data-driven approach, institutions can implement programs and support systems that better address the needs of students, helping them to stay on course for graduation.

Another crucial application of BI is the early identification of at-risk students. Predictive analytics within BI platforms allow institutions to monitor student performance and engagement in real-time, identifying those who may be falling behind academically or facing personal challenges. By recognizing these students early on, educators and administrators can deploy targeted intervention strategies to provide the necessary support. This might include academic tutoring, mentoring programs, mental health resources, or financial assistance. BI not only helps to identify these



A. A. Aziz et al., *Business Intelligence for Higher Education*,
https://doi.org/10.1007/978-3-032-05361-9_6

students but also tracks the effectiveness of the intervention strategies in place, providing insights that can refine and optimize support mechanisms.

Moreover, BI plays a key role in measuring and evaluating student performance on a granular level. Through customized dashboards and detailed reports, institutions can track key performance indicators (KPIs) such as GPA trends, course completion rates, retention of course material, and participation in extracurricular activities. This data is invaluable for both students and educators, offering a clear view of academic progress and areas that need improvement. For administrators, these insights can guide institutional decisions, such as adjusting curricula, allocating resources more effectively, or tailoring instructional methods to better suit the needs of the student population. By continuously measuring and evaluating student performance through BI metrics, institutions can foster an environment that prioritizes academic success and continuously adapts to the evolving needs of students.

BI also enables schools to monitor and evaluate the effectiveness of various academic programs and institutional initiatives. By assessing how different programs impact student success, schools can make informed decisions about where to invest resources or how to reshape curricula. Whether it's tracking how students in specific disciplines perform over time or measuring the outcomes of retention initiatives, BI allows for a comprehensive evaluation that leads to more informed, strategic planning. Therefore, the following subchapter will discuss one of our case studies how BI can be used to enhance students success.

## 6.2 Implementing BI for Student Success (Malaysian Case Study for ICT Sector)

### *6.2.1 Talent Management (TM) Problems*

The notable growth in Malaysia's ICT sector and the dynamism in the global IT ecosystem have created a huge demand for talents in the respective domain. However, inconsistent supply of graduates from Malaysian Institutes of Higher Learning (IHLs) and deficiency in industry relevant skills among them resulted in a gap between talent demand and supply. Despite many IHLs offering ICT courses, aligning the right courses to industrial needs with the aim to strike a balance between supply and demand is not an easy task. This problem can be attributed to:

- Lack of centralized repository of quality assured information about talents that can facilitate comprehensive analysis of what we have and what we need to have concerning graduates to allow appropriate measure of improvement.
- Lack of integration of information about ICT talents across IHLs in Malaysia, with trending industrial needs in a single repository to provide information that can facilitate TM practices such as mapping of talents to industrial needs.

Therefore, there is a critical need for a platform that integrates, harmonizes, and consolidates big data related to ICT talents from diverse sources alongside current industry demands. Such a platform would facilitate the creation of a national talent pool based on student academic performance and provide an advanced reporting system utilizing appropriate business intelligence tools to enhance talent management practices.

This project aims to develop a BI system that intuitively matches talents to relevant industry needs. The focus of the research is on designing the data warehouse component of this BI system. In this context, the study takes into account the IT industry requirements in computer science as identified by the Multimedia Development Corporation (MDEC). The industry's outlined needs are based on job vacancies in 2014 among IT companies registered under the Malaysia Status Companies (MSC) program. Additionally, the research considers academic performance data of graduates from the Faculty of Informatics and Computing (FIK) at Universiti Sultan Zainal Abidin (UniSZA), Malaysia.

### 6.2.2 Talent Management Data Warehouse Model (TMDW)

This is the first stage of DW development. It involves the choice of the subject on which the DW will be built. It concerns the understanding of the business needs and data requirements of the users of the system. This is achieved through careful evaluation of the available data in consideration of user requirements. In order to accomplish successful warehouse development, the problem to be solved (user requirement) must be considered and the information needed to solve the problem (and its various sources) must be identified. Requirements gathering therefore are very much oriented toward understanding the problem domain for which the modeling will be done.

Therefore all the relevant data sets associated with the research components have to be obtained and analyzed. This study consists of two major components namely Talent and Industrial Needs. Each of these components has a set of data associated with it. The Fig. 6.1 illustrates the data sets involved in the study.

The first set of data is a structured data (secondary data) of students' academic performance from an existing Student Information System. In addition, this study considers an operational database of student information from Faculty of Informatics and Computing (FIK), Universiti Sultan Zainal Abidin. The database contains a list of students, their program (diploma or degree), their specialization, courses offered, respective grades and CGPA. Secondly, the other set of data is also secondary data of current Industrial Needs. The focus of the research is on ICT industrial needs, thus, a list of ICT jobs was obtained from Multimedia Development Corporation (MDeC) Malaysia. According to MDEC classification, Malaysia ICT sector is divided into three clusters: Information technology, Creative multimedia (CMC), and Shared Services and Outsourcing (SSO) clusters respectively. For the purpose of this study, consideration was given to industrial needs (available jobs) with

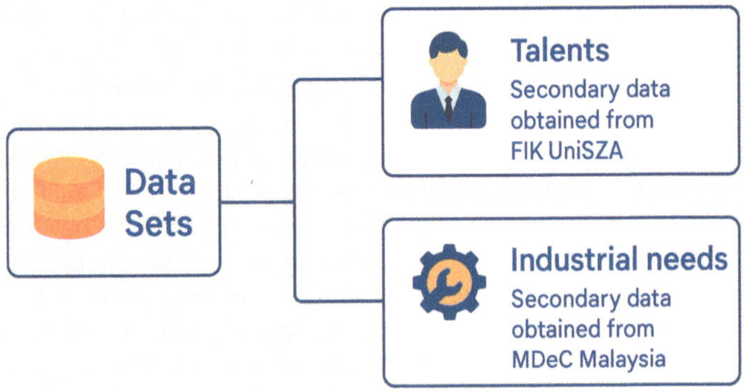


**Fig. 6.1** Data sets

highest vacancies from MSC registered companies as at 2014 across all the clusters. Furthermore, this research only considers jobs that are available for entry level. (This implies that any job that requires special experience or certification among the listed jobs in the MDeC report is not considered).

In order to define the system requirement in this study, the student data was thoroughly analyzed to understand the attributes that constitute the talent. Also, to find out which ones are relevant with regards to the industrial needs and define the specification of the proposed DW. However, the data was analysed based on two key elements. These elements are the subject that is being analyzed and the evaluation criteria. The examined subject (Talent) represents a dimension and the analysis criteria (academic performance) represent the measure.

Firstly, the dimensions that apply to each fact row are chosen. The available data is thoroughly evaluated to identify and choose the multidimensional concepts that will form the DW from the potential dimension and measures specified in the previous phase. However at this stage, any entity within the collected data that can be used to analyze talent is chosen. Hence, corresponding dimensions include the student (talent), attributes and other related entities with regards to the application domain. These entities include institutions attended; the years spent, the subjects offered the program and so forth.

Secondly the fact is identified. A set of dimensions and their associated measures makes a fact. Further, facts usually contain numerical values of performance indicators or measure. In this regard the corresponding Marks scored per subject and Grade Point Average (GPA) are the indicators that measure performance of a student. Hence, they will serve as the measures. Usually end-user requirements at this stage are documented rather informally or at least they are not represented in detailed schemas.

**Table 6.1** List of jobs with highest vacancies in IT cluster

| Information technology cluster (IT) | |
|---|---|
| S/N | Job title |
| 1 | Software Engineer |
| 2 | Net Programmer |
| 3 | Java Programmer |
| 4 | PHP Programmer |
| 5 | C/C++ Programmer |
| 6 | Customer Support Engineer |
| 7 | Technical Support Engineer |
| 8 | Team Lead |
| 9 | Solution Architect |
| 10 | IT Sales Engineer |
| 11 | Software QA Engineer |
| 12 | SAP Consultant |
| 13 | Contact Centre Agent Inbound |
| 14 | IT Business Analyst |
| 15 | System Architect |
| 16 | Java Consultant |

**Table 6.2** List of jobs with highest vacancies in SSO cluster

| Shared services and out-sourcing cluster (SSO) | |
|---|---|
| S/N | Job title |
| 1 | Technical Helpdesk Analyst |
| 2 | Contact Centre Agent Inbound |
| 3 | Java Programmer |
| 4 | Customer Support Engineer |
| 5 | Contact Centre Agent Outbound |
| 6 | Net Programmer |
| 7 | Technical Support Engineer |
| 8 | Software QA Engineer |
| 9 | SAP Consultant |
| 10 | Contact Centre Recovery Staff |
| 11 | Contact Centre Business Analyst |
| 12 | Accounting Analyst |
| 13 | Network Engineer |
| 14 | Software Engineer |
| 15 | Team Lead |
| 16 | C/C++ Programmer |

### 6.2.3 *Designing Fact Tables and Dimension Tables*

The list was collected from the Multimedia Development Corporation (MDeC) report. The Tables 6.1, 6.2 and 6.3 below is the list of Job titles with highest vacancies as at 2014 by Information Technology, Shared Services and Outsourcing, and Creative Multimedia Clusters respectively.

**Table 6.3** List of jobs with highest vacancies in CMC cluster

| Creative multimedia cluster CMC | |
|---|---|
| S/N | Job title |
| 1 | Animator |
| 2 | Digital Artist |
| 3 | 3D Modeler |
| 4 | Game Designer |
| 5 | Compositor |
| 6 | Visual Effects Artist |
| 7 | Graphic Designer |
| 8 | Storyboard Artist |
| 9 | CG Artist |
| 10 | Editor |
| 11 | Game Programmer |
| 12 | Lighting Artist |
| 13 | Creative Director |
| 14 | Render Wrangler |
| 15 | Web Designer |
| 16 | Producer 1 |

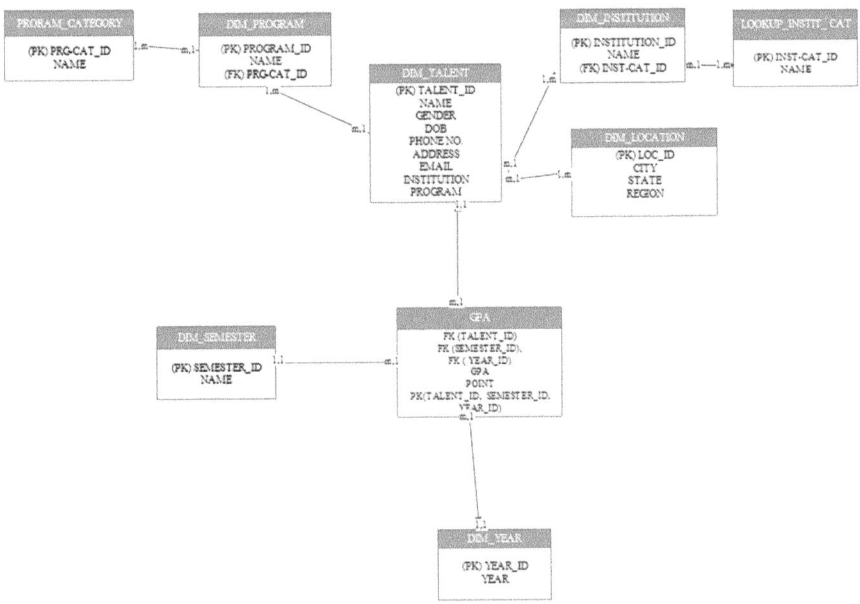


**Fig. 6.2** FACT_GPA

Based on the specification and defined procedure, two Fact schemas, FACT_GPA and FACT_MARK were generated as shown in Figs. 6.2 and 6.3 below respectively.

However, these two fact tables can stand as independent data marts as each provide information of different atomicity. The Marks data mart contains information of students' performance per course, and the GPA contains the student

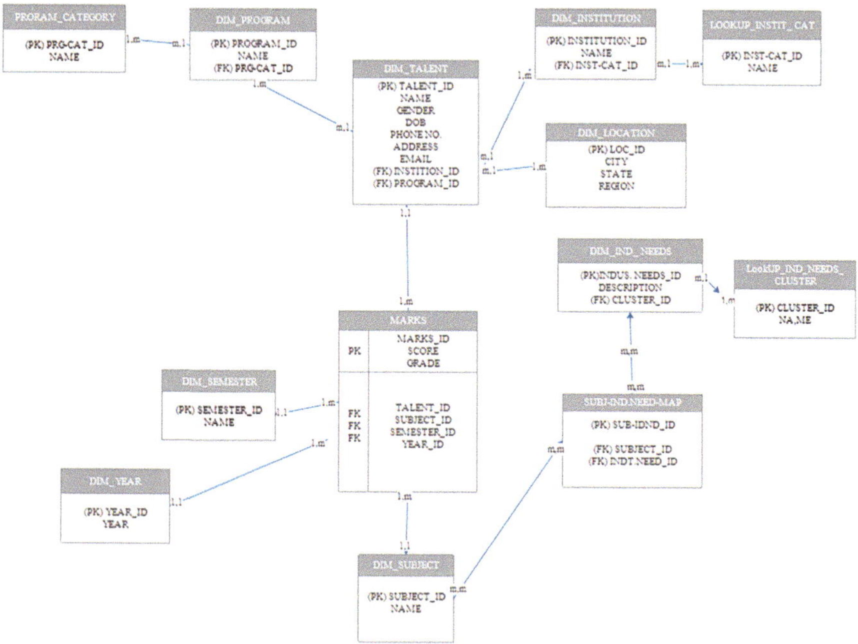


**Fig. 6.3** FACT_MARKS

performance per semester, which will determine the class of his qualification as at graduation (that is excellent, good, pass or fail). These two independent data marts will give a more detail information about a student that will enable HR managers to choose the best candidate for a particular job. The rationale behind having these two data marts with each containing student performance but in different granularity is that; Employers usually have a cut-off class of qualification, say a good class in diploma or second -class upper in degree to be eligible for a particular job. However, a candidate might have such qualification in his overall CGPA but fail the core course required for available job. Therefore, information about his score in individual courses he offered is needed to know the strength of that candidate. For example, an employer in need of programmer requires someone with a good result in computer science or information technology. However, a candidate might have good result in the above courses but have a week grade in programming which is the pre-requisite requirement for the job. Therefore, the CGPA data mart will indicate the strength of the candidate qualification, and the marks data marts will indicate the strength of the candidate in individual courses he offered. Moreover, these two data marts are joined together to form a larger DW to provide all the information at different atomicity. The Fig. 6.4 below is the DW model inform of star schema.

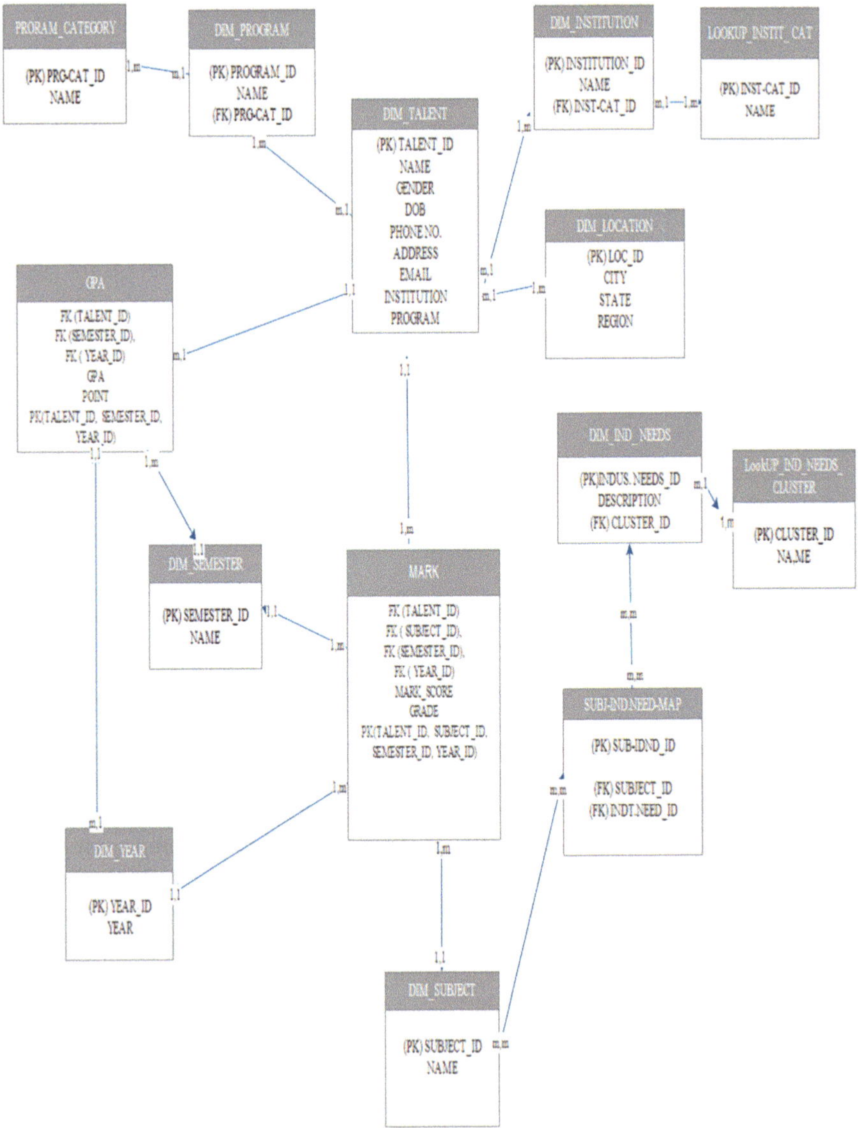


**Fig. 6.4** TMDW schema

### 6.2.4 *Reporting*

This analysis as represented in Fig. 6.5 provides us with talents academic performance on courses related to any selected industrial needs. Two filters were applied to drill down on the data. These filters are talents qualification (Degree or Diploma) and Industrial Needs. Talents academic performances are displayed on the

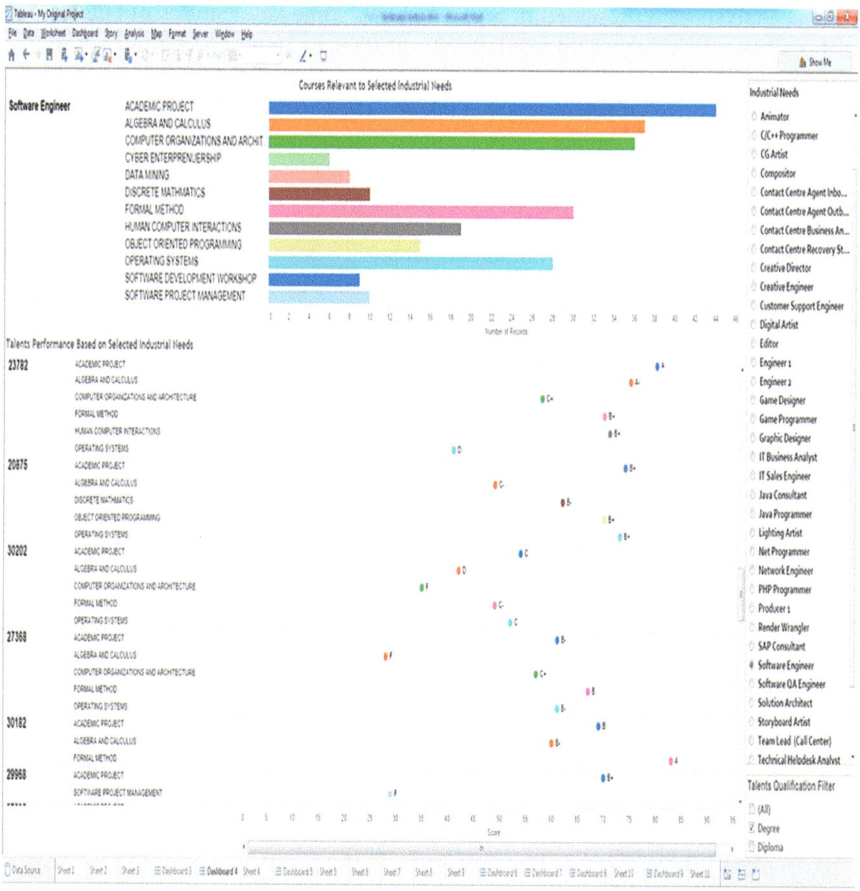


**Fig. 6.5** Descriptive analysis showing talents academic performance for a selected industrial need

dashboard with data visualization on talents grade and courses related to the selected industrial needs. The data sets used in this analysis are:

- Score: Measure from talents-performance
- Subject: Dimension attribute from subject identifier table
- Grade: Measure from talents-performance table
- Program Cluster: Dimension attribute from program cluster look-up table
- Reg No: Dimension attribute from talents table
- Industrial Needs: Dimension attribute from industrial needs table

From the analysis carried out, it can be understood that the industrial needs of a Software Engineer should include good academic performance in those subjects mapped to Software Engineer. Furthermore, based on the industrial need selected, only talents that took courses mapped to Software Engineer were shown with their respective performance and grade in each course.

This analysis as represented in Fig. 6.5 shows some key features of talents. The analysis was carried out with a synchronized filter of Program of Study. With the selection of a single or multiple program of study, the dashboard updates each section with descriptive information about talents. The key features of talents displayed include talents CGPA, talents contact details, talents institution, talents institution segment (Public, Private, or Community College), and talents qualification (Degree or Diploma). The data sets used in this analysis are:

- CGPA: Measure attribute from talents table
- Program: Dimension attribute from program look-up table
- Phone: Dimension attribute from talents table
- Reg No: Dimension attribute from talents table
- Institution: Dimension attribute from institution look-up table
- Institution Cluster: Dimension attribute from institution cluster look-up table
- Email: Dimension attribute from talents table

From the analysis carried out, the talent with the registration number 23966 has the highest CGPA mark of 3.8. Furthermore, we can deduce that the talent has a (B.Sc.) degree qualification (Fig. 6.6).

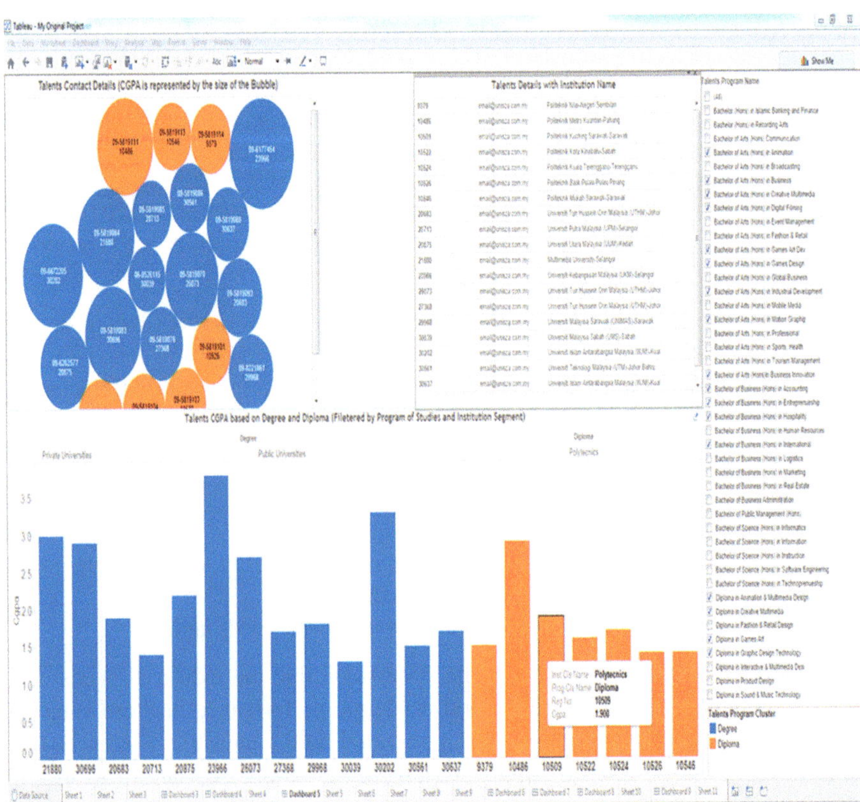


Fig. 6.6 Descriptive analysis showing talents key feature

## 6.3 Chapter Conclusion

In this chapter, we explored the transformative role of Business Intelligence (BI) in Data Visualization and Reporting within higher education, particularly in enhancing student success. The ability to analyse, visualize, and report on educational data is crucial for institutions striving to improve retention rates, graduation rates, and overall academic performance. BI serves as a powerful tool for data-driven decision-making, enabling educators and administrators to identify trends, predict student outcomes, and implement targeted interventions.

A key benefit of BI discussed in this chapter is its role in improving student retention and graduation rates. By leveraging BI tools, institutions can analyse enrolment trends, attendance records, and engagement metrics to detect patterns associated with student attrition. These insights allow universities to take a proactive approach by implementing personalized support systems and academic interventions before students disengage or drop out.

Another major application of BI is the early identification of at-risk students. Predictive analytics enables real-time monitoring of academic performance, participation levels, and external challenges. Institutions can use these insights to deploy targeted support strategies, such as mentorship programs, academic tutoring, financial aid, and mental health resources. The continuous tracking of intervention effectiveness ensures that data-driven strategies remain adaptive and responsive to students' evolving needs.

Furthermore, BI allows institutions to evaluate student performance and academic programs with greater granularity. By using customized dashboards and interactive reports, stakeholders can monitor key performance indicators (KPIs) such as GPA trends, course completion rates, and program effectiveness. These insights not only enhance student learning experiences but also assist administrators in resource allocation, curriculum design, and institutional policymaking.

The Malaysian Case Study on Talent Management in the ICT Sector further demonstrated BI's significance in bridging the gap between higher education and industry needs. The Talent Management Data Warehouse Model (TMDW) showcases how BI can be applied to align graduates' skills with market demands, ensuring a steady supply of well-trained ICT professionals. By integrating academic performance data with industry job requirements, BI provides a strategic framework for talent mapping, workforce planning, and policy formulation.

# Chapter 7
# Privacy, Security, and Ethical Considerations

## 7.1 Introduction

In today's digital age, big data, and business intelligence (BI) have become indispensable tools for organizations to make informed decisions, optimize operations, and drive innovation. However, the use of BI also raises privacy, security, and ethical considerations, particularly in the context of higher education institutions. Privacy refers to the right of individuals to control the collection, use, and disclosure of their personal information. In higher education, student data is a valuable resource for BI, but it also contains sensitive information such as academic records, financial data, and health information. Institutions must ensure that they obtain consent from students for the collection and use of their data and provide transparency about how it will be used and protected.

Security refers to the measures taken to prevent unauthorized access, theft, or misuse of data. Higher education institutions must implement robust security protocols to safeguard student data from cyber threats and data breaches and ensure that access to sensitive data is restricted to authorized personnel only. This includes regular data backups and disaster recovery plans to mitigate the impact of data loss or corruption.

Ethical considerations involve the social, moral, and legal implications of using BI in higher education. Institutions must ensure that they use BI to promote educational equity, access, and opportunity, and avoid perpetuating disparities based on race, gender, or socioeconomic status. They must also ensure that BI is used to enhance student learning and outcomes, rather than as a tool for surveillance or disciplinary action.

Higher education institutions can harness the power of BI to drive informed decision-making while safeguarding the rights and interests of students, faculty, and other stakeholders. This requires a commitment to privacy, security, and ethical



A. A. Aziz et al., *Business Intelligence for Higher Education*,
https://doi.org/10.1007/978-3-032-05361-9_7

considerations, and a proactive approach to addressing the challenges and opportunities presented by BI in higher education.

Privacy, security, and ethical considerations are closely intertwined when safeguarding student and institutional data in a Business Intelligence (BI) environment. Safeguarding student and institutional data in a Business Intelligence (BI) environment is crucial to maintain trust, comply with regulations, and protect sensitive information. Higher education establishments can create a safe BI environment while guarding institutional and student data against breaches, illegal access, and other security risks.

## 7.2 Safeguarding Student and Institutional Data in a BI Environment

In a BI (Business Intelligence) context, safeguarding student and institutional data refers to the procedures and policies higher education institutions put in place to keep private information safe from theft, unauthorised access, and abuse. This covers sensitive data during testing and development operations or training sessions, data classification, access control, encryption (both at rest and in transit), data masking, and anonymization. Institutions should also put procedures in place for data backup and recovery to guarantee data availability in the event of data loss or corruption. Along with promoting data security awareness among staff and students through regular training sessions, they should also have policies in place for data usage and sharing that respect data privacy and protection. Organisations need to have a plan in place for responding Protecting student and institutional data within a Business Intelligence (BI) environment involves implementing robust strategies to ensure that sensitive information remains secure from unauthorized access, misuse, or breaches. As BI tools and processes are used for data analysis and decision-making, it becomes essential to establish comprehensive safeguards that uphold data privacy and security.

Key considerations include:

- Data Privacy: Ensuring that student and institutional data is collected, processed, and used in compliance with relevant privacy regulations and policies. This includes obtaining informed consent, anonymizing or pseudonymisation personally identifiable information (PII), and limiting data access to authorised users.
- Data Security: Implementing robust security measures to protect data against unauthorised access, data breaches, and cyber threats. This includes encryption of data at rest and in transit, access controls, authentication mechanisms, intrusion detection systems, and regular security audits.
- Ethical Data Use: Upholding ethical principles in the collection, analysis, and use of student and institutional data. This involves mitigating biases in data analysis, ensuring transparency and accountability in data handling practices, and

using data to enhance student outcomes and institutional effectiveness responsibly.

- Compliance: Ensuring compliance with relevant data protection regulations such as GDPR, CCPA, FERPA, and HIPAA, depending on the nature of the data collected and the jurisdiction of the institution. Compliance involves adhering to legal requirements, implementing data governance frameworks, and maintaining documentation of data handling practices.
- Risk Management: Identifying and mitigating risks associated with data handling and BI processes to prevent potential security incidents or data breaches. This includes conducting risk assessments, implementing controls to mitigate identified risks, and developing incident response plans.
- Training and Awareness: Providing training and raising awareness among employees, students, and stakeholders about data privacy, security best practices, and ethical considerations. Educating users about their rights and responsibilities regarding data protection promotes a culture of data security and privacy awareness.

Safeguarding student and institutional data in a BI environment require a holistic approach that addresses privacy, security, ethics, compliance, risk management, and user awareness to ensure the confidentiality, integrity, and availability of data while leveraging BI tools and insights to support informed decision-making and improve educational outcomes. Safeguarding student and institutional data in a BI environment is crucial for higher education institutions to maintain trust with their stakeholders, protect sensitive information, and avoid reputational damage.

Institutions may effectively protect student and institutional data while encouraging trust, compliance, and responsible data stewardship by including privacy, security, and ethical considerations in the design, implementation, and governance of BI systems. By implementing these best practices, higher education institutions can safeguard student and institutional data in a BI environment, promote data security awareness, and avoid reputational damage. Let's explore how each aspect relates to ensuring data protection and some best practices for safeguarding student and institutional data:

### *7.2.1 Privacy*

Data Minimization: Privacy concerns emphasise the importance of collecting and storing only the necessary data for BI purposes. Minimising data collection reduces the risk of exposure and potential harm to individuals if a breach occurs.

Anonymization and Pseudonymization: To protect individual privacy, sensitive information such as personally identifiable information (PII) should be anonymized or pseudonymized whenever possible. This ensures that individuals cannot be directly identified from the data.

Informed Consent: Respecting individuals' privacy rights involves obtaining informed consent before collecting and processing their data for BI purposes. Transparency about data usage and providing individuals with control over their data promotes trust and compliance with privacy regulations.

### 7.2.2 Security

Access Controls: Security measures like role-based access control (RBAC) restrict access to sensitive data, ensuring that only authorised users can view or manipulate it. Implementing strong authentication mechanisms further strengthens data security.

Encryption: Encrypting data at rest and in transit prevents unauthorised access or interception of sensitive information. Encryption algorithms ensure that even if data is compromised, it remains unintelligible without the proper decryption keys.

Regular Audits and Monitoring: Continuous monitoring and regular security audits help detect and respond to security threats in real-time. Monitoring user activities, network traffic, and system logs enables early detection of anomalies or unauthorised access attempts.

### 7.2.3 Ethical Considerations

Bias Mitigation: Ethical BI practices involve ensuring that data analysis and decision-making processes are free from biases that could unfairly disadvantage certain groups. Implementing measures to identify and mitigate biases in data collection, analysis, and reporting promotes fairness and equity.

Responsible Use of Data: Ethical guidelines dictate that data should be used responsibly and for legitimate purposes. BI insights should be used to enhance student outcomes, improve institutional operations, and support informed decision-making, while avoiding misuse or exploitation of data for unethical purposes.

Transparency and Accountability: Ethical considerations emphasise the importance of transparency and accountability in data handling practices. Institutions should be transparent about their data policies, practices, and the purposes for which data is collected and used. Establishing accountability mechanisms ensures that individuals or entities responsible for data management are held accountable for their actions.

By integrating privacy, security, and ethical considerations into the design, implementation, and governance of BI environments, institutions can effectively safeguard student and institutional data while promoting trust, compliance, and responsible data stewardship.

## 7.3 Best Practices for Safeguarding Student and Institutional Data

Safeguarding student and institutional data is essential for fostering trust, meeting regulatory requirements, and defending against the growing landscape of cyber threats. Higher education institutions must adopt a multifaceted approach that combines robust governance, advanced technical safeguards, secure networks, and a strong culture of user awareness. By integrating these elements, institutions can significantly reduce the risk of data breaches and unauthorized disclosures. Regular security audits, proactive risk management, and well-established compliance frameworks further strengthen the institution's ability to respond to threats in an increasingly digital academic environment.

Prioritizing data protection is not just about compliance—it is about preserving the privacy and security of all members of the academic community. With the constant evolution of cyber risks, educational institutions must stay current with emerging security trends and continually update their protocols to mitigate potential vulnerabilities. Investing in comprehensive data protection strategies is fundamental to upholding institutional integrity, reputation, and operational resilience.

Key components of a holistic data protection framework include:

- **Data Classification:** Institutions should systematically categorize data according to sensitivity—such as public, internal, confidential, or restricted. This classification enables targeted protection measures, ensuring that the most sensitive information receives the highest level of security and compliance oversight.
- **Data Access Control:** Adopting role-based access control (RBAC) policies ensures that individuals can access only the data necessary for their job functions. By aligning data access with organizational roles, institutions can minimize the risk of unauthorized exposure and misuse of sensitive data.
- **Data Encryption:** Encrypting data both at rest (stored data) and in transit (data being transferred between systems) is crucial. Encryption acts as a protective barrier, making it extremely difficult for unauthorized parties to interpret or misuse the data even if a breach occurs.
- **Data Masking:** Data masking involves obscuring specific data elements—such as student IDs or financial details—during development, testing, or training scenarios. This prevents sensitive information from being exposed in non-production environments while allowing necessary activities to proceed.
- **Data Anonymization:** Through anonymization techniques, personally identifiable information (PII) is removed or altered, ensuring that individuals cannot be identified even if data is accessed without authorization. This approach is particularly important when using data for research or analytics.
- **Data Backup and Recovery:** Regularly backing up data and maintaining a disaster recovery plan ensures that information remains available and recoverable in case of accidental loss, corruption, or cyber incidents such as ransomware attacks.

- **Data Privacy and Protection Policies:** Institutions should establish clear policies governing how data is collected, stored, shared, and disposed of. These policies ensure that all data handling practices are transparent, ethical, and compliant with relevant privacy laws and standards.
- **Data Governance:** Implementing comprehensive data governance practices helps maintain high standards of data quality, accuracy, and consistency. Governance structures set clear accountability for data stewardship and establish procedures for data lifecycle management.
- **Data Security Awareness:** Providing ongoing training and awareness programs for faculty, staff, and students promotes best practices in data security. Well-informed users are less likely to fall victim to phishing, social engineering, or other security threats.
- **Data Breach Response Plan:** Developing and regularly updating a data breach response plan enables institutions to act swiftly and effectively in the event of a data incident. This includes predefined steps for containment, investigation, notification, and recovery, minimizing the impact of any breach.

Compliance with data protection laws—such as the General Data Protection Regulation (GDPR) or Malaysia's Personal Data Protection Act (PDPA)—is vital. Adhering to these regulations not only protects student privacy but also enhances institutional reputation, avoids costly legal penalties, facilitates responsible data sharing and collaboration, and supports effective data-driven decision-making. By embedding these practices into the fabric of institutional operations, higher education organizations can build a secure, resilient, and trusted digital environment for all stakeholders.

## 7.4 Compliance with Data Protection Regulations (e.g., GDPR, HIPAA)

Compliance with data protection laws is a critical requirement for any organization that collects, processes, or stores personal data—including higher education institutions. These legal frameworks, such as the General Data Protection Regulation (GDPR) in Europe and the Health Insurance Portability and Accountability Act (HIPAA) in the United States, are specifically designed to safeguard the privacy, rights, and freedoms of individuals. They set clear expectations for how organizations must handle personal information, mandating responsible, ethical, and transparent data practices at every stage of the data lifecycle.

For higher education institutions, adherence to these laws is not simply a matter of avoiding penalties, it is about demonstrating a genuine commitment to the protection of sensitive student and staff data. Personal information managed by universities often includes not only academic records but also financial, health, and behavioral data. Mishandling such information can lead to serious privacy violations, loss of trust, legal consequences, and reputational damage.

Key elements of compliance include obtaining informed consent before collecting data, limiting data use to specific, legitimate purposes, ensuring data accuracy, enabling individuals to access or correct their information, and maintaining secure systems to prevent unauthorized access or breaches. Institutions are also required to report data breaches promptly and take corrective measures to mitigate any impact.

Integrating compliance into Business Intelligence (BI) initiatives brings additional benefits. By embedding data protection principles into the design and implementation of BI systems, institutions can responsibly analyze and leverage student and institutional data to drive better decision-making. For example, anonymized or pseudonymized data can be used in analytics projects to uncover patterns in student performance or resource utilization without exposing individual identities. This not only minimizes privacy risks but also supports a culture of transparency and accountability.

Moreover, compliance with regulations such as GDPR and HIPAA helps foster trust among students, faculty, staff, parents, and external stakeholders. When individuals know their personal data is handled with care and integrity, they are more likely to engage with institutional systems and participate in initiatives that rely on accurate data collection and reporting. Trust is especially important in the education sector, where long-term relationships and reputational standing are vital to institutional success.

By proactively aligning BI practices with data protection laws, higher education institutions can reduce the risk of costly data breaches, avoid regulatory penalties, and strengthen their reputation as responsible data stewards. Most importantly, this approach ensures that data-driven insights—gained through robust and compliant BI analysis—translate into meaningful improvements in student support, operational efficiency, and institutional effectiveness.

Compliance with data privacy regulations like GDPR and HIPAA is not just a legal obligation but a strategic imperative. It is essential for protecting the rights of individuals, building institutional credibility, and fully realizing the transformative potential of Business Intelligence in the modern educational landscape.

### *7.4.1 Information*

Compliance with data protection regulations such as GDPR (General Data Protection Regulation) and HIPAA (Health Insurance Portability and Accountability Act) is crucial for higher education institutions when implementing business intelligence (BI) initiatives. Here's how these regulations intersect with privacy, security, and ethical considerations in BI for higher education:

#### 7.4.1.1 Data Protection Principles

The GDPR establishes core principles for the lawful processing of personal data, including lawfulness, fairness, transparency, purpose limitation, data minimization, accuracy, storage limitation, integrity, and confidentiality. For higher education institutions implementing BI initiatives, this means:

- **Lawfulness and Fairness:** BI tools and data analytics must process data in ways that are legal and just. This requires that data collected for educational, administrative, or research purposes is only used for those explicit, legitimate purposes.
- **Transparency:** Institutions must be transparent about what data they collect, how it is used in BI applications, and for what purposes. This involves clear privacy notices and regular communication with students, faculty, and staff.

#### 7.4.1.2 Lawful Basis for Processing

Before utilizing BI tools to analyze personal data, higher education institutions must establish a lawful basis for processing under GDPR. The most relevant bases for higher education BI use cases include:

- **Consent:** Obtaining explicit consent from data subjects for the use of their data in analytics projects, such as surveys or research studies.
- **Contractual Necessity:** Processing data as part of fulfilling contractual obligations to students or staff, such as managing academic records or financial transactions.
- **Legitimate Interests:** When processing is necessary for the legitimate interests of the institution (such as institutional research or student support analytics), provided these interests do not override the fundamental rights and freedoms of individuals.

#### 7.4.1.3 Data Subject Rights

GDPR empowers individuals (data subjects) with significant rights over their personal data, and institutions must have systems in place to uphold these rights in all BI processes:

- **Right of Access:** Individuals have the right to know what personal data is held about them and how it is being processed or analyzed.
- **Right to Rectification:** If data is inaccurate or incomplete, data subjects can request corrections.
- **Right to Erasure ("Right to be Forgotten"):** Data subjects may request the deletion of their personal data under certain conditions, such as when it is no longer necessary for the purpose it was collected.

- **Right to Restrict Processing and Object:** Individuals can limit or object to how their data is used in BI analytics, especially if the use is for profiling or marketing.

Institutions must establish responsive mechanisms and workflows for handling such requests promptly and effectively.

#### 7.4.1.4 Data Transfers Outside the EEA

When personal data must be transferred beyond the European Economic Area (EEA)—for example, to cloud-based BI service providers or research partners—GDPR mandates the use of appropriate safeguards:

- **Standard Contractual Clauses (SCCs):** Legally binding agreements that require non-EEA entities to protect personal data in line with EU standards.
- **Adequacy Decisions:** Recognizing that the recipient country has adequate data protection measures, allowing for free and secure data transfers.
- **Binding Corporate Rules (BCRs):** Internal policies adopted by multinational institutions for data transfers within the same organization.

Institutions must carefully vet third-party vendors and ensure that cross-border data transfers do not compromise the privacy or security of students and staff.

## 7.5 Chapter Conclusion

In this chapter, we explored the critical aspects of privacy, security, and ethical considerations in the Business Intelligence (BI) environment for higher education. As institutions increasingly rely on data-driven decision-making, safeguarding student and institutional data has become a fundamental responsibility. Ensuring data security, regulatory compliance, and ethical data usage is essential to maintaining trust, protecting sensitive information, and upholding institutional integrity.

One of the primary challenges discussed was data privacy and security in a BI ecosystem. Higher education institutions handle vast amounts of sensitive data, including student records, financial information, and academic performance metrics. Implementing robust cybersecurity measures, encryption techniques, and access control policies is crucial in preventing data breaches, unauthorized access, and cyber threats. A well-structured data governance framework ensures that institutions can balance data accessibility with security, allowing stakeholders to derive insights while protecting confidential information.

We also examined the importance of compliance with data protection regulations, such as the General Data Protection Regulation (GDPR), the Health Insurance Portability and Accountability Act (HIPAA), and other regional privacy laws. These regulations establish legal obligations for institutions to safeguard personal data, enforce transparency in data processing, and provide individuals with control over their information. Compliance with these frameworks not only mitigates legal risks but also fosters ethical responsibility in managing student data.

Additionally, ethical considerations in BI applications were explored, particularly in relation to analyzing student data. While BI tools provide valuable insights into student behavior, academic performance, and institutional efficiency, their use must be governed by ethical principles such as fairness, accountability, and transparency. The potential risks of algorithmic bias, data misuse, and surveillance concerns were highlighted, emphasizing the need for responsible AI and data ethics policies. Institutions must ensure that BI-driven decisions do not unfairly disadvantage students, violate privacy, or create inequitable educational outcomes.

# Chapter 8
# Future Trends in BI for Higher Education

## 8.1 Introduction

Future trends are predicted changes, improvements, or shifts in numerous facets of a certain sector or business. These trends are likely to arise or become more significant in the future, depending on current trends, technological advancements, changing consumer behaviors, market dynamics, and other relevant variables. Identifying and analyzing future trends enables people, organizations, and industries to plan for future changes, adjust their strategy, and remain competitive in an ever-changing world. In Higher Education, future trends in BI are related to advancements and developments that are specifically tailored for use in higher education environments. These trends comprise emerging technologies, processes, and practices that are expected to shape the future landscape of BI integration and utilization in academic institutions. Future trends in BI for higher education may include the use of sophisticated analytics methods, a greater emphasis on predictive analytics, the incorporation of AI and ML technologies, enhanced data visualization capabilities, and the development of more personalized and adaptable BI solutions tailored to the unique needs of educational institutions. Future trends may also include improvements in data governance and security protocols, increased collaboration and data exchange among institutions, and the use of BI tools to support strategic initiatives and decision-making processes at both the institutional and individual levels in higher education.



A. A. Aziz et al., *Business Intelligence for Higher Education*, https://doi.org/10.1007/978-3-032-05361-9_8

## 8.2 Emerging Technologies in Higher Education

Emerging technologies represent some of the most recent innovative tools and breakthroughs in BI in higher education, which are particularly developed for deployment in universities and colleges. These technologies cover cutting-edge developments designed specifically for higher education institutions, with the intention of further enhancing data analytics and decision-making processes in this sector. A few examples of new technology in business intelligence for higher education may include:

### *8.2.1 Artificial Intelligence (AI) and Machine Learning (ML)*

AI and ML are advanced computing techniques that allow computers to simulate the intelligence of humans, accomplish activities that would normally need human cognition, and transform higher education. These technologies are critical in allowing data-driven decision-making, personalizing learning experiences, and optimizing administrative operations in order to enhance student achievement and institutional effectiveness. Besides, AI algorithms and machine learning models are used to analyze large datasets, forecast student outcomes, personalize learning experiences, and improve administrative operations. In higher education, these technologies are used in a variety of ways:

- **Analysing Large Volumes of Data**: It entails reviewing large datasets from many sources inside educational institutions, such as student records, academic performance measurements, and administrative information. This study is made feasible by AI algorithms and machine learning models that efficiently process vast volumes of data. This study allows AI to find hidden patterns, trends, and correlations that human analysts may miss. By disclosing these insights, AI helps educational institutions better grasp complicated data linkages, allowing for more informed decision-making and strategic planning.
- **Predicting Student Outcomes:** It requires the implementation of AI and ML approaches to generate prediction models for various aspects of student performance and behavior in educational environments. These models can anticipate academic performance, retention rates, and graduation probabilities. These prediction models are developed by analyzing previous data on student demographics, behaviors, academic achievement, and other appropriate characteristics. This data may contain information about students' backgrounds, socioeconomic status, prior academic achievements, attendance records, engagement levels, and extracurricular activities, among other things. Predictive models are capable of predicting which students would struggle academically or drop out according to their history, previous grades, and activity. Early identification of these students will allow institutions to provide targeted assistance to improve their achievement. Using AI and ML in predicting student outcomes will enable institutions

to identify and address possible student concerns ahead of time, hence increasing success rates and overall institution performance.

- **Personalizing Learning Experiences:** AI-powered adaptive learning platforms leverage ML algorithms to personalize educational content and activities based on individual student needs, preferences, and learning styles. These platforms analyze student interactions with learning materials to dynamically adjust the content and pace of instruction, providing customized learning experiences tailored to each student's abilities and learning objectives.
- **Optimizing Administrative Processes:** In educational institutions, it entails using AI and ML technologies to automate and simplify processes such as admissions, course scheduling, and resource allocation. These tools analyze historical data and learn from previous decisions to offer insights and recommendations for improving administrative procedures. AI and ML technologies boost productivity by automating regular processes such as admissions application processing and course scheduling. Furthermore, these technologies can analyze data to detect trends and patterns, allowing organizations to make more informed judgements regarding resource allocation and strategic planning. In this regard, AI-powered systems may analyze previous enrollment data to predict expected student demand for courses, allowing institutions for optimal course scheduling in order to satisfy student demands while minimizing wasteful use of resources. Furthermore, AI algorithms are able to analyze budget and resource utilization data to discover the areas where resources are being insufficiently utilized or might be better reassigned. As a whole, AI and ML technologies improve administrative processes at educational institutions by automating duties, offering insights for decision-making, and boosting operational efficiency, thus increasing the institution's overall efficacy.

### *8.2.2 Predictive Analytics*

It refers to the exploitation of statistical algorithms and machine learning techniques to analyze previous data and forecast future occurrences or trends. Predictive analytics are utilized in higher education to estimate different outcomes such as enrollment patterns, student success rates, graduation rates, and resource allocation based on future demands. Besides, it may assist institutions in forecasting future enrollment trends by analyzing historical data on enrollment patterns, student demographics, academic performance, and other pertinent variables. This allows them to better plan and deploy resources to meet the requirements of the incoming students. Furthermore, predictive analytics is valuable to identify at-risk students by analysing data on their historical academic achievement, engagement levels, and any other factors. By identifying these students promptly, the institutions may provide tailored support mechanisms to increase their chances of success. Predictive analytics also enables forecasting the graduation rates from the historical data on student progress and completion rates analysis. This makes it possible for institutions to identify hurdles of graduation and devise strategies to improve student retention and completion rates. Basically, prediction analytics is a new technology that is implemented in higher education that uses data analysis and prediction modelling as guidance in decision-making, improving student outcomes, and allocating resources for future demands.

### *8.2.3 Natural Language Processing (NLP)*

Using NLP technology, users may engage with BI systems using natural language queries, enabling easier data exploration and analysis for non-technical users. This technology eliminates the need for users to have in-depth knowledge of complex query languages and allows them to simply ask questions in their own words. It also enhances the speed and efficiency of data analysis, enabling users to quickly retrieve insights and make informed decisions. Furthermore, NLP technology offers a more intuitive and user-friendly experience, as it understands context and can interpret ambiguous queries. This means that users can receive accurate and relevant results even if they are not familiar with the exact terminology used in the data. Additionally, this technology allows for easier collaboration and communication among users, as they can easily share their queries and findings with others in a clear and concise manner. Overall, leveraging NLP technology in BI systems greatly enhances the accessibility and usability of data analysis, empowering non-technical users to take advantage of the power of data-driven insights.

### *8.2.4 Augmented Reality (AR) and Virtual Reality (VR)*

Integrating AR and VR technologies into business intelligence (BI) dashboards and reporting tools includes implementing current technology into the interfaces and tools functionality. The objective is to improve on how the data is visualized and presented to the people. Users may have a more immersive and engaging experience with data visualization through the implementation of AR and VR technology. Instead of viewing data on a standard two-dimensional screen, users may interact with it in three dimensions or in a virtual environment where data points are represented as interactive objects or elements within the space around them. They may be able to employ and interact with these data points using gestures or controllers, providing a more intuitive and engaging way to analyze information. This provides the opportunity for a more comprehensive and intuitive data analysis, allowing users to obtain deeper understandings and make more informed decisions. Besides, the integration of both AR and VR opens up new possibilities for data exploration and analysis, as users can manipulate and examine data from different angles and perspectives. With AR, users can overlay data onto the real world, making it easier to understand and interpret complex data sets. On the other hand, VR creates fully immersive environments where users can dive deep into data visualizations and gain insights in a more engaging and interactive manner. Ultimately, the integration of AR and VR into BI dashboards and reporting tools revolutionizes the way data will be presented and understood, enhancing decision-making processes and driving innovation in various industries.

### *8.2.5 Blockchain Technology*

Blockchain is an immutable distributed digital ledger that safely logs transactions via a computer network. In order to improve data integrity and transparency inside higher education institutions, it has been investigated for safe data sharing, credential verification, and student records management. Within the discipline of higher education, this inquiry involves exploring the ways in which blockchain technology might be utilized towards achieving several goals:

- Secure Data Sharing: Traditional data sharing methods often rely on centralized servers or databases. These central points of control can be vulnerable to cyberattacks or unauthorized access. In contrast, blockchain operates on a decentralized network, where copies of the data are distributed across multiple nodes or computers. This decentralized nature makes it extremely difficult for a single entity to manipulate or compromise the data. Therefore, this situation will assist in improving the security of data and remains secure from unauthorized access or tampering. In the context of educational institutions, blockchain can be used to create a secure and transparent system for sharing data. It's essential to protect the educational documents such as student transcripts and certificates, as they are confidential and must be shielded from unauthorized viewing or tampering. The built-in security aspects of blockchain technology guarantee that any recorded data remains unchangeable and undeletable without being noticed. For example, a university can utilize blockchain technology to securely share student records with potential employers. Instead of relying on a central database vulnerable to hacking, the university can store student records on a blockchain network that requires consensus from multiple nodes to validate any changes made. This ensures that employers receive accurate and tamper-proof information about the students' academic achievements and qualifications.
- Credential Verification: In a higher education context, blockchain technology can be used to verify the authenticity of academic credentials, such as degrees or certifications, by creating a tamper-proof record of academic achievements on the blockchain. This enhances the trustworthiness and reliability of credential verification processes by eliminating the possibility of falsification or manipulation of academic credentials. It also simplifies the verification process and reduces administrative burdens for educational institutions and employers. Additionally, it enhances the overall efficiency and accuracy of credential verification. Lastly, it promotes trust and confidence in the validity of academic quali-

fications, improves the hiring process for employers, and streamlines the admissions process for educational institutions. Overall, using a tamper-proof and secure credential verification system makes sure that people's academic credentials accurately reflect who they are. This not only benefits employers by ensuring they are hiring qualified candidates but also saves time and resources for educational institutions by automating the verification process. Ultimately, it creates a more transparent and reliable ecosystem where academic achievements are validated, fostering a stronger and more trustworthy workforce.

- Student Records Management: The utilization of blockchain technology can enhance the efficiency of managing student data by securely storing academic records, transcripts, and other relevant information on the blockchain. This system offers clear and verifiable documentation of a student's academic background, which can be easily retrieved and confirmed when required. This system has the potential to revolutionize the way educational institutions handle student data and ensure the accuracy and transparency of academic history records. It can greatly streamline administrative processes and eliminate the risk of fraud or tampering. Additionally, it can significantly enhance the efficiency and effectiveness of data management in educational institutions. The records that are preserved on the blockchain can be accessed more easily and verified quickly. Educational institutions, potential employers, or other authorized entities can verify a student's academic credentials without having to go through lengthy and manual verification processes. This system can be especially beneficial for verifying the credentials of students who have studied at multiple institutions or in different countries. Moreover, it can streamline administrative processes and provide valuable insights for decision-making. In summary, using blockchain technology in student records management can enhance the security and confidentiality of sensitive student information. This approach also has the potential to significantly reduce administrative burdens and enhance the integrity of academic credentials.

In higher education institutions, the exploration of blockchain technology seeks to improve the reliability and transparency of data by utilizing the built-in security and unchangeable nature of blockchain. This is done to ensure the credibility of data sharing, credential verification, and student records management in institutions. By implementing blockchain technology, higher education institutions can create a decentralized system that eliminates the need for intermediaries, making data sharing more efficient and cost-effective. Additionally, the immutability of blockchain ensures that student records cannot be tampered with, providing a secure and trustworthy platform for credential verification. Ultimately, the adoption of blockchain technology in higher education institutions has the potential to revolutionize data management and enhance the overall integrity of the education system.

### 8.2.6 Data Virtualization

Data virtualization is a technological solution that enables organizations to retrieve and control data from several sources without the need for physical relocation or duplication. Instead, it generates a virtual layer that offers a consolidated perspective on information from several sources. Implementing data virtualization techniques in this context refers to the use of this technology for the purpose of managing data integration. Educational institutions commonly store data in several systems and formats, including databases, spreadsheets, cloud services, and other platforms. These sources may not always be compatible or readily accessible. Data virtualization enables smooth integration and immediate access to data from many sources in real-time. These approaches enable institutions to establish a singular and consolidated perspective on their data. This implies that all pertinent data from various sources is presented in a coherent and structured fashion. This comprehensive viewpoint facilitates comprehension of the entirety of institutional data. To summarize, the statement highlights the significance of utilizing developing technologies, such as data virtualization, in the realm of BI. Through this approach, educational institutions may effortlessly include data from several sources in real-time, resulting in a comprehensive and cohesive perspective of their data. The consolidated data can thereafter be utilized for comprehensive analysis and reporting, ultimately facilitating well-informed decision-making within the organization. By leveraging data virtualization, educational institutions can overcome the challenges of data silos and integrate information from various sources seamlessly. This not only allows for a holistic view of institutional data but also enables faster and more accurate decision-making. With comprehensive analysis and reporting capabilities, institutions can identify trends, patterns, and outliers, leading to more informed strategies and improved outcomes. Ultimately, the adoption of developing technologies like data virtualization empowers educational institutions to stay competitive and adapt to the ever-changing landscape of higher education.

### 8.2.7 Cloud-Based BI Solutions

Adopting cloud-based BI solutions for scalability, flexibility, and cost-effectiveness, allowing higher education institutions to access and analyse large volumes of data without significant infrastructure investments.

"Cloud-based BI Solutions" refers to Business Intelligence (BI) software and tools that are hosted and delivered through cloud computing infrastructure. In the context you provided, it is specifically referring to the use of such solutions in higher education institutions. Here's a breakdown of the key components:

Cloud-based BI Solutions: These are software and services designed for analysing and reporting on data related to an organization's operations. Instead of running on a local server or on-premises infrastructure, these BI solutions are hosted in the cloud, which means the software and data are stored and processed on remote servers managed by a third-party cloud provider, such as Amazon Web Services (AWS), Microsoft Azure, or Google Cloud Platform (GCP).

Adopting cloud-based BI solutions: This phrase suggests that higher education institutions are making a deliberate decision to implement and use cloud-based BI tools. They are moving away from traditional on-premises BI systems, which may be limited in terms of scalability, flexibility, and cost-effectiveness.

## 8.3 Predictions of BI Future in the Academic Sector

The future of Business Intelligence (BI) and Analytics in academia will be shaped by the rapid evolution of technology, institutional needs, and global educational trends. Universities and educational institutions are increasingly adopting BI tools, big data analytics, artificial intelligence (AI), and cloud computing to enhance decision-making, improve student outcomes, and streamline administrative processes. As the demand for data-driven insights grows, institutions will need to adapt to new technologies that enable real-time analytics, predictive modelling, and personalized education experiences.

One of the key areas of transformation is student success and retention. With the help of predictive analytics, universities can identify at-risk students and implement early intervention strategies to improve graduation rates. By analysing historical and real-time student data—such as academic performance, attendance, and engagement levels—BI tools can provide actionable insights that help educators tailor support systems for students. Similarly, online and hybrid learning environments will further drive the need for learning analytics to monitor course effectiveness, student participation, and overall engagement in virtual classrooms.

Data privacy and security will also play a crucial role in the future of BI in academia. With growing concerns over cybersecurity threats and regulatory compliance (such as GDPR, HIPAA, and other data protection laws), institutions will need to implement strict security measures to safeguard student and institutional data. This includes adopting encryption techniques, access control policies, and ethical AI frameworks to ensure responsible data usage. Additionally, bias in algorithms and ethical concerns surrounding data-driven decision-making will require universities to develop clear governance policies and guidelines for responsible BI adoption.

Another significant trend is the integration of AI-powered insights into educational decision-making. AI-driven analytics can optimize resource allocation, improve curriculum development, and enhance institutional performance metrics. Through the use of automated dashboards, machine learning algorithms, and natural language processing (NLP), universities can gain deeper insights into academic trends, faculty performance, and student learning behaviors. Furthermore, collaboration and interoperability between universities and BI solution providers will lead to the development of integrated platforms that allow for cross-institutional data sharing and benchmarking.

The increasing importance of data literacy and training will also shape the future of BI in higher education. As institutions embrace data-driven culture, there will be a growing emphasis on teaching students and faculty how to analyze, interpret, and utilize BI insights effectively. This shift may lead to the integration of data analytics courses into academic curricula to prepare future professionals for careers in data science, business analytics, and AI-driven industries.

Additionally, the future of BI in academia will be influenced by funding and resource allocation. Universities will need to weigh the return on investment (ROI) when implementing BI initiatives, considering factors such as cost-effectiveness, infrastructure requirements, and long-term sustainability. Furthermore, sustainability analytics is emerging as a key area where BI can contribute, helping institutions track and reduce their carbon footprint, energy consumption, and environmental impact.

From a global perspective, the adoption of BI and analytics in higher education will vary across different regions based on technological infrastructure, policy frameworks, and institutional priorities. Some universities in developed nations may lead in AI-powered BI adoption, while institutions in developing regions may focus on building foundational BI systems to improve data accessibility and reporting capabilities.

In conclusion, the future of BI and Analytics in academia is poised for significant growth, with technological advancements, data-driven strategies, and ethical considerations shaping its trajectory. Universities that invest in cutting-edge BI tools, AI-driven analytics, and strong data governance frameworks will be better positioned to enhance academic excellence, improve student success, and optimize institutional decision-making. However, as BI continues to evolve, institutions must remain adaptable, ensuring that their data practices align with security standards, ethical principles, and the changing landscape of higher education.

## 8.4 Chapter Conclusion

The future of Business Intelligence (BI) in higher education is driven by technological advancements such as AI, predictive analytics, and cloud computing, enabling institutions to make more data-driven decisions that enhance student outcomes, resource allocation, and overall efficiency. Personalized learning, real-time student monitoring, and predictive analytics will play a pivotal role in improving retention rates and academic performance by identifying at-risk students and offering timely interventions.

At the same time, institutions must address data privacy, security, and ethical concerns as BI tools become more integrated into decision-making processes. Compliance with GDPR, HIPAA, and other data protection regulations will be critical in ensuring responsible data use while mitigating biases in AI-driven analytics.

Furthermore, AI-powered BI tools will enhance strategic planning, faculty performance evaluation, and curriculum development, enabling universities to optimize operations and align academic programs with industry demands. Data literacy initiatives will become essential, equipping students and educators with the skills to leverage analytics for research and decision-making. BI will also play a role in sustainability efforts, helping institutions monitor energy consumption and reduce environmental impact.

In conclusion, the future of BI in higher education lies in leveraging intelligent analytics, prioritizing ethical data governance, and fostering a data-driven culture. Institutions that embrace these innovations will be better positioned to drive academic excellence, operational efficiency, and long-term sustainability.

# References


Abelló, A., Golfarelli, M., Mazón, J. N., & Rizzi, S. (2023). *Data warehouse systems: Design and implementation* (2nd ed.). Springer. https://doi.org/10.1007/978-3-031-18704-1

Arnold, K. E., & Pistilli, M. D. (2012). Course signals at Purdue: Using learning analytics to increase student success. In *Proceedings of the 2nd International Conference on Learning Analytics and Knowledge* (pp. 267–270).

Bouzeghoub, M., & Kedad, Z. (2002). Quality in data warehousing. In M. G. Piattini, C. Calero, & M. Genero (Eds.), *Information and database quality* (Advances in database systems) (Vol. 25, pp. 163–185). Springer. https://doi.org/10.1007/978-1-4615-0831-1_8

Chen, H., Chiang, R. H. L., & Storey, V. C. (2012). Business intelligence and analytics: From big data to big impact. *MIS Quarterly, 36*(4), 1165–1188.

Daniel, B. (2015). Big data and analytics in higher education: Opportunities and challenges. *British Journal of Educational Technology, 46*(5), 904–920.

De Waal, A. A. (2013). *Strategic performance management: A managerial and behavioural approach*. Palgrave Macmillan.

Eckerson, W. W. (2010). *Performance dashboards: Measuring, monitoring, and managing your business*. Wiley.

Golfarelli, M., & Rizzi, S. (2020). *Data warehouse design: Modern principles and methodologies* (2nd ed.). McGraw-Hill.

Inmon, W. H. (2005). "Building the Data Warehouse," Wiley Publishing, Inc., Hoboken.

Kaplan, R. S., & Norton, D. P. (1996). *The balanced scorecard: Translating strategy into action*. Harvard Business School Press.

Kimball, R., & Ross, M. (2019). *The data warehouse toolkit: The definitive guide to dimensional modeling* (3rd ed.). Wiley.

Kumar, V., et al. (2021). Cloud data warehousing: Architecture, features, and trends. *Journal of Cloud Computing, 10*(1), 1–19. https://doi.org/10.1186/s13677-021-00261-9

Long, P., & Siemens, G. (2011). Penetrating the fog: Analytics in learning and education. *Educause Review, 46*(5), 31–40.

Marr, B. (2015). *Key performance indicators: The 75 measures every manager needs to know*. Pearson.

Parmenter, D. (2015). *Key performance indicators: Developing, implementing, and using winning KPIs*. Wiley.

Picciano, A. G. (2012). The evolution of big data and learning analytics in American higher education. *Journal of Asynchronous Learning Networks, 16*(3), 9–20.

Suriyapperuma, K., & Kahandawaarachchi, C. (2022). Leveraging data warehousing for higher education analytics: A case study. *International Journal of Educational Technology in Higher Education, 19*, 24. https://doi.org/10.1186/s41239-022-00347-2





A. A. Aziz et al., *Business Intelligence for Higher Education*,
https://doi.org/10.1007/978-3-032-05361-9